THE SECRET HISTORY OF

JANE EYRE

The first page of Charlotte Brontë's manuscript for Jane Eyre, *sent to the publishers*
Smith, Elder in August 1847. © GRANGER

THE SECRET HISTORY OF

JANE EYRE

*How Charlotte Brontë Wrote
Her Masterpiece*

JOHN PFORDRESHER

W. W. NORTON & COMPANY
INDEPENDENT PUBLISHERS SINCE 1923
NEW YORK   LONDON

Material from *The Brontës* © Juliet Barker, published by Pegasus Books,
has been used with permission.

Charlotte Brontë: The Evolution of Genius by Winifred Gerin (1969).
By permission of Oxford University Press.

For information about permission to reproduce selections from this book, write to
Permissions, W. W. Norton & Company, Inc., 500 Fifth Avenue, New York, NY 10110

For information about special discounts for bulk purchases, please contact
W. W. Norton Special Sales at specialsales@wwnorton.com or 800-233-4830

Manufacturing by LSC Communications Harrisonburg
Book design by JAM Design
Production manager: Lauren Abbate

Library of Congress Cataloging-in-Publication Data

Names: Pfordresher, John, author.
Title: The secret history of Jane Eyre : how Charlotte Brontë
wrote her masterpiece / John Pfordresher.
Description: First edition. | New York : W. W. Norton & Company, [2017] |
Includes bibliographical references and index.
Identifiers: LCCN 2017013160 | ISBN 9780393248876 (hardcover)
Subjects: LCSI I: Brontë, Charlotte, 1816–1855. Jane Eyre. |
Brontë, Charlotte, 1816–1855—Authorship.
Classification: LCC PR4167.J5 P46 2017 | DDC 823/.8—dc23
LC record available at https://lccn.loc.gov/2017013160

W. W. Norton & Company, Inc.,
500 Fifth Avenue, New York, N.Y. 10110
www.wwnorton.com

W. W. Norton & Company Ltd.,
15 Carlisle Street, London W1D 3BS

1   2   3   4   5   6   7   8   9   0

For Sissy Seiwald

How dare I? Because it is the *truth*.

Contents

Introduction

We begin with a mystery. Let's imagine that it is October 19, 1847.

A new book has just been published in London. The first reviews are rapturous.

On October 23 the *Atlas* finds the novel has "all the freshness and some of the crudeness of youth about it," and yet credits the author with a knowledge of "the profoundest springs of human emotion," the kind of wisdom usually achieved only after "years of bitter experience." The critic, while enthusiastic, is clearly curious about the identity of the author. Is this writer young or old? Freshly youthful or seasoned by years of difficulties overcome? The review then proclaims that this "is one of the most powerful domestic romances" to have appeared in many years. It's an innovative work, with "little or nothing of the old, conventional stamp upon it." Indeed, summing up, the *Atlas* concludes that this "tale of passion" is "a book to make the pulses gallop and the heart beat, and to fill the eyes with tears."

But where did this book—so unlike the work of the known writers of the day—come from?

Curious readers would find on its laconic title page the following: "Jane Eyre. An Autobiography. Edited by Currer Bell."

Who were these two people? Even the book's publisher, Smith, Elder, didn't know. And was it an "autobiography"? The *Atlas* called it a powerful domestic romance. Was it fact or fiction?

The relationship of the publishers at Smith, Elder in London with the author was conducted entirely by post. They found themselves writing to someone from Haworth, a small town in the north of England, who signed correspondence "C Bell"; the replies from London were to be delivered "Under cover to Miss Brontë."

For half a year, during months of growing success for the book, the mystery continued. Speculation was rife—A man or a woman? Young or old?—nobody knew who this Bell person was, or whether this was an edited autobiography or a work of fiction.

Then a disreputable London publisher named Newby floated a rumor that he had the manuscript of a new Currer Bell novel soon to be published. Needless to say this troubled the people at Smith, Elder, who then wrote the author asking what was going on. A day later, two young women from Yorkshire, a little staggered after an all-night train ride, arrived on the morning of Saturday, July 8, 1848, at Smith, Elder's London offices. Charlotte and Anne Brontë stood before them. *Jane Eyre*, it seemed, was not an edited autobiography, but a novel, written by Charlotte.

This was not the end of the story. Charlotte Brontë took her editors into her confidence but insisted on maintaining her identity secret. Despite the efforts of the London literati, she largely succeeded in keeping it a mystery until the end of 1850.

Then, in a "Biographical Notice" prefacing new editions of

Wuthering Heights and *Agnes Grey*, Charlotte, in mourning for her lost sisters, divulged that the authors of those two novels were, respectively, Emily Brontë, who had died December 19, 1848, and Anne Brontë, who had died May 28, 1849. In Charlotte's words, "The little mystery, which formerly yielded some harmless pleasure, has lost its interest; circumstances are changed." The phrase "little mystery" suggests that her wish to conceal her authorship was a playful whim. Actually, matters were far more complicated.

Now that readers knew that Currer Bell was actually Charlotte Brontë, how much could they learn about her? More to the point, how might one account for the ability of this reclusive young woman, living in isolation in the West Riding of England, to write an utterly new and powerful "tale of passion"? And furthermore, what was the relationship of the author, called "Editor" on the novel's title page, to the character Jane Eyre?

Brontë denied that there were significant similarities between her life and that of her first-person narrator and heroine. In a particularly funny episode, as late as May 29, 1851, William Makepeace Thackeray enraged her when at the end of a public lecture he cried out, "Mother, you must allow me to introduce you to Jane Eyre!" Charlotte was so angered by his very public announcement that she was the author of the novel and that the protagonist and narrator were based on her, that she sought out Thackeray the next afternoon to upbraid him. Her publisher, George Smith, accidentally walked in on them as she was dressing down the celebrated author of *Vanity Fair* and was amazed, as he put it, by "[t]he spectacle of this little woman, hardly reaching to Thackeray's elbow, but, somehow, looking stronger and fiercer than himself, and casting her incisive words at his head, resembled the dropping of shells into a fortress."

The vehemence of her denial was nothing new. Throughout the months after *Jane Eyre* first appeared, Charlotte persistently lied about her authorship. In May of 1848 her dear friend Ellen Nussey relayed to Charlotte that she heard a rumor that Charlotte had published something. She replied venomously that to say so would be "an unkind and an ill-bred thing." She insisted that "profound obscurity" was infinitely preferable to a "vulgar notoriety" and that she repelled and denied every such "accusation." Charlotte's language voices an angry fear. Why would suggesting she has written a book be an "accusation"? How might being the author of a popular novel imply that she was guilty of something? The "little mystery" appears, at moments such as this, immensely important to Charlotte; important enough for her to threaten Ellen that anyone who says she has published is "no friend of mine."

If she was so concerned about preserving her anonymity that she lied about the publication of the novel to close friends, why did Charlotte Brontë write *Jane Eyre* in the first place? And why was she so keen on maintaining the secret of her relationship to the novel?

There are many reasons. Perhaps the most important is that this was a book born from a series of calamities that led to a crisis in Brontë's life: what she called "an almost unbearable inner struggle." Her heart, "constantly lacerated by searing regrets," led Brontë to the discovery that "[o]ne suffers in silence so long as one has the strength and when that strength fails one speaks without measuring one's words too much." In *Jane Eyre* Brontë found those words, a way to voice her struggle and her pain. She seized upon those things that had hurt, shamed, angered, and compelled her, as well as those desires that she could not control, and transformed them into a fiction which was so profoundly intimate that this publicly reserved, proper, and proud young woman didn't want anyone to know they were hers. In the pages that follow, we will learn how and why she did this, and as we do, we will come to understand more completely some of the sources for this novel's compelling power, something felt by its first readers 170 years ago, and felt still by twenty-first-century readers.

THE SECRET HISTORY OF

JANE EYRE

I

Secret History

In the summer of 1846 there was an immediate crisis that Charlotte Brontë had to face. Due to cataracts, her father was going blind. In order to understand why this was so calamitous, one must know a little bit about her unusual family.

Patrick Brontë, as a Church of England parish priest, enjoyed a small but permanent income; a large rectory that was home for his children, sister-in-law, and servants; and the social status that made him a leader in his community. His wife had died early, as had the two oldest girls, leaving only his sister-in-law to help raise the four surviving children.

As they grew, the Brontë children—Charlotte, Emily, Anne, and Branwell—enjoyed a happy and secure childhood living in the Haworth parsonage. Since there was no suitable school nearby, their father tutored them according to age and ability. They read everything they could get their hands on, indulging in their father's fairly extensive library and his subscriptions to regional newspapers, as well as national periodicals such as *Blackwood's Edinburgh Magazine,* which they borrowed from friends. Exuberant and playful, the children rambled by themselves in the miles of open moorland beyond their house. Separated by class status from the local people, they lived an isolated life.

Crucial to all four was the constant writing of fiction and poetry. Its initiation was Patrick's gift to Branwell in June 1826—a box of toy soldiers. At the time, Charlotte was ten, Branwell nine, Emily eight, and Anne six. The children seized upon these tiny figures as a basis for ever-expanding, collaboratively imagined fantasy worlds. Gathered at a large common table, they wrote stories in pairs: Emily with Anne, Branwell with Charlotte. The children created histories and chronicles—tales of dynastic struggles, romance and reckless bravery—drew maps and, later, portraits of favorite characters, and also wrote magazines about these imagined worlds, which even included pretend advertisements. Because their fiction was supposed to be "by" the toy soldiers, they fashioned tiny manuscripts using a miniscule print that replicated the printed page; these sometimes began with title pages, details about imaginary book publishers, and sale prices. They sedulously stitched together the pages to make toy-sized books and continued producing them until well into their early adult years. From 1827 when she was eleven, until at least 1839 when she was twenty-three, Charlotte shared in this collaborative writing. In the end Charlotte and Branwell produced hundreds and hundreds of pages of pseudo-historical narratives, poetry, and fiction. The emotional intimacy and intensity of this practice offered Charlotte the greatest happiness of her young life. It created an alternative world that she often found far more deeply involving—and in that sense "real"—than everyday experience. The same was true for her brother and sisters.

When the Brontë children reached maturity, it was time for them to find work to help support the family and their now aging father. In this they failed. Charlotte, when she was nineteen, and Anne, when she was twenty, got brief jobs as governesses; Emily, at twenty, taught for some months in a boarding school for girls, but all soon returned home. Branwell, also at age twenty, tried being a tutor in the home of a clergyman, had a love affair with the lady of the house, and was expelled.

Back home, they all continued to dream of success as writers, but, with the exception of a few poems by Branwell that appeared in local newspapers, none of them could find publishers for their work. The sisters self-published a collection of their poems. Two copies were sold.

Now, all of them were threatened by Patrick's blindness. If Patrick lost his eyesight, he lost his post as parish priest, lost the rectory that was the family home, and lost his standing as a leader in the community. And with his children seemingly incapable of earning money, how would they survive? This then was the family crisis.

As the oldest daughter, Charlotte felt responsible for rescuing the family. She took it upon herself to care for her father's health: finding him a specialist in Manchester willing to operate on his eyes and setting a date for the operation.

As Charlotte was managing this and its strain, she was experiencing a second, entirely secret, and intensely personal crisis. Several years earlier, in February 1842, hoping to win financial independence for the family by starting their own school, Charlotte and her sister Emily set off for Brussels to learn French, thinking they could use this skill to attract students. There Charlotte, twenty-six-years old, fell in love with Constantin Heger, the husband of the woman running the school. Returning home in January of 1844, Charlotte began writing passionate letters to him, which first met with an alarmed and distant response, and then silence.

Haunted by those "searing regrets," Charlotte took her father to Manchester in August 1846. During the days and weeks following the operation, while her father rested his eyes in an adjoining darkened room, she started writing the novel that would become *Jane Eyre*.

As she began to write, what could she have hoped for?

Certainly money, to fulfill her responsibilities to protect and sustain her family. Indeed, she was to continue to carry on this role until her death. Her younger brother, who should have traditionally taken on this burden, proved incapable of ever holding a paying job. Pride dictated she not speak of these matters with others. Although she was concerned, once she had sold the book, about sales, her contractual relationship with her publisher, and her writing's commercial success, Charlotte assiduously sought to keep financial matters private.

The other hope? The further reason for writing?

As we shall see in detail in Chapter Seven, the secret letters to Constantin Heger probably ended in November of 1845. The unstated hope driving the writing of *Jane Eyre*, which she began drafting nine months later, was in all likelihood to create a novel of romantic love that would achieve—through imagination—the fantasy fulfillment of an adulterous passion that was never to be hers. But, at least in her novel, Brontë could have her heroine voice her feelings, addressing them not to Heger but to the fictional Fairfax Rochester: "All my heart is yours . . . and with you it would remain were fate to exile the rest of me from your presence forever." Jane's words, but Charlotte's defiant message. Here, certainly, was a strong reason for Brontë to maintain her fierce insistence that she was not the source for her heroine.

And yet, what else did Charlotte have to draw upon as she began to write this book, given her limited experience of life and of people? Indeed, she saw herself lacking, as she later wrote, that "knowledge of the world, whether intuitive or acquired" enjoyed by the "eminent writers" of the day. How was she to create the highly detailed world of this novel, with its story of dangerous and passionate love, and its spiky, independent-minded, risk-taking heroine?

She turned inward. Ironically, *Jane Eyre* was indeed, as the seemingly mysterious title page proclaimed, an autobiography, drawn both from Brontë's personal experiences and also from a rich and long-standing fantasy life that emerged from the books she had read and the shared writing she and Branwell had created. These should be private matters, and Victorian propriety dictated silence. And yet, because this was really all she had, Brontë had no choice, in the late summer of 1846, but to write about herself.

She was well aware of what she was doing. In a letter dated November 6, 1847, still using her pseudonym "C Bell," she discussed the two very different sources she had used for her novel. She was addressing G. E. Lewes, a writer only a year younger than she, whose novel *Ranthorpe* had just published. In the weeks after Brontë's novel first appeared, Lewes was preparing a review of *Jane Eyre* for the December *Fraser's Magazine*. This letter is one of the most crucial documents we have telling us how consciously Brontë understood her work as a writer of fiction—and its relationship to her life. She begins by responding to a cautionary observation Lewes had voiced in an earlier, now lost, letter to her. "You warn me to beware of Melodrama" she writes, "and you exhort me to adhere to the real." Doubtless Lewes had been referring to not only the highly emotional, and hence melodramatic, moments in *Jane Eyre* but perhaps as well to scenes that stretched the limits of credibility, as when Jane seems to hear Mr. Rochester crying out to her in despair—from a great distance—at the moment when she seems ready to promise marriage to another man. Charlotte argues that her initial intent had been to avoid melo-dramatic extremes and to write just the sort of realistic novel, based on actual experience, which Lewes was exhorting. "When I first began to write," Brontë recalls, "so impressed was I with the truth of the principles you advocate that I determined to take Nature and Truth as my sole guides and to follow in their very footprints." And for this reason she carefully "restrained imagination, eschewed romance; repressed excitement . . . and sought to produce something which would be soft, grave and true." But, she continues, she soon began to worry that to write this way constantly, to be an unremitting realist depending solely on her own experience, particularly given that this experience was "very limited," not only risked the danger of tedious repetition, but also that the writer might become "an egotist." Here we see this key anxiety of Brontë's emerging. She doesn't wish to push herself too much into the foreground. Though she doesn't tell this to Lewes, she knows how much of her past life is in her novel and how that could possibly lead not only to tedium but also to exposure, which she feared. And so, rather teasingly, she moves to the second source for her book: not experience, but imagination; not realism, but fantasy. She concedes that a new demand emerged. "Imagination is a strong, restless faculty which claims to be heard and exercised, are we to be quite deaf to her cry and insensate to her struggles? When she shewes us bright pictures are we never to look at them and try to reproduce them?" Here, though she would never dream of revealing the truth, Brontë alludes to the many crucial and powerful moments in *Jane Eyre* that depict not those things she had experienced, but rather the "bright pictures" of those things she longed for. It's telling, and significant, that Brontë gives imagination a feminine gender. It is *she* who is strong and restless, who cries out and struggles to be heard. For Brontë the answer to her rhetorical question is clear: the dreams of desire have their own rights.

The success *Jane Eyre* enjoyed from its earliest days owes to Charlotte Brontë's conscious awareness that, from the start, this is how she will work: Truth and Imagination, realism and fantasy each given their proper function in the creation of the whole. Both are intensely personal for her: the truth of her experience and the emotionally dominant claims of her imagination. And both, as she could not say to Lewes, are far too intimate for her to admit that they are hers.

In the pages that follow, we will explore these twin sources of Brontë's remarkable achievement. While she insisted that her invented protagonist had little relationship to her own life, in fact, just about everything that the novel reveals about Jane comes from Charlotte's experience. Indeed, the title page is—perhaps intentionally—quite accurate: this is "An Autobiography," but one transformed into a novel.

It is thus a book with a "secret history." In one of the novel's most amazing and self-revealing moments, near the end of the narrative, Brontë writes about this very topic, self-consciously and wittily presenting it in Chapter XXIX. A young, and very attractive clergyman, St. John Rivers, trying to help Jane, whom he has found near death from exhaustion, quizzes her about her past. Where did she come from? Whom did she know? Though she is at the moment totally dependent upon the sympathy of Rivers and his sisters, Jane crisply replies, "The name of the place where, and of the person with whom I lived, is *my secret* . . . " He presses her: "Yet if I know nothing about you or *your history*, I cannot help you . . . " Still, she stiffly preserves her silence. Her heroine is never more like Brontë than in this moment when Jane demands to keep *her* history secret. The novel's heroine and the woman who invented her will face their crises alone, eschewing the help of others.

Indeed, in this impulse to secrecy, Jane replicates one of the most autobiographical heroines of Brontë's earlier writings— Elizabeth Hastings in the novella *Henry Hastings*—which she had written back in 1839. Characterized as "a being made up of intense emotions," which, "in her ordinary course of life [she] always smothered under diffidence and prudence," persisting in the struggle "to keep wrapt about her the veil of reserve and propriety." This, as we shall find in a wide variety of examples, is one of the dominant characteristics of Brontë's personality. She was a woman who, most of the time, concealed her emotional life behind a mask of severe English "reserve and propriety." But the passionate intensity was always there.

In the pages to follow we will explore the dynamics of Brontë's secret history. Her genius was to mingle memory and its forms of "truth" with the claims of imagination. In virtually every part of *Jane Eyre* we will see both.

The truth of memory is itself a complex problem.

In *Jane Eyre* Brontë takes the reader to the past "facts" of her own life. For example, to the Cowan Bridge School, where her father fondly and impractically sent her in 1824 when she was only eight years old. There she witnessed the sudden crisis in health that led to the deaths of her two older sisters Maria and Elizabeth. She draws upon her adolescent educational experience of 1831–1832 at a private school for girls where she met two of her lifelong friends, and her later return to that same school as a teacher from 1835 to 1838. She recalls her intensely unhappy experience working as a governess (1839, 1841). And, crucially, she returns to her life in Brussels from 1842–1843, a culturally alien environment where nevertheless she excelled as a student even as she was falling disastrously in love with her tutor.

A "very limited" life from one point of view, little more than domestic scenes from a parsonage and the daily trivia of schools for girls—what, Brontë might have asked herself, is there in this kind of remembered "truth" to interest a reader? But Brontë's novel uses what she recalls in a very personal way. Her memory transforms what we know to actually have happened into scenes of intense feeling and high drama alternating with equally touching moments of relief, tranquility, and affection. Everything is felt and rendered in terms of the emotions not only of the moment recalled but also of the moment when in remembering they are transcribed into narrative. For example, in *Jane Eyre* Charlotte describes a clergyman, administrator of a school for girls, as "a black pillar," a "narrow, sable-clad shape," a "carved mask." This is how Charlotte Brontë, writing in 1846, remembered an actual man encountered in August of 1824 when she was age eight. His friends, still alive when the novel was published, were enraged at the depiction. But this is the truth of a child's memory recalled by a grown and indignant woman, the kind of experiential truth Brontë was using, and which her letter to Lewes insists has its own validity.

There are other, similarly highly personal and private sources for *Jane Eyre*. Brontë was an inexhaustible reader, and any consideration of her fiction must explore the impact reading had on her vision of the world and its meaning. Living in the home of Diana and Mary Rivers, Jane Eyre "devoured the books they lent me" and relished the "full satisfaction" found in discussing them in the evening.

Walter Scott's poem *Marmion*, then a "new publication," announced for them "the golden age of modern literature," and in her words we hear Jane Eyre's excitement in the discovery of a new writer. That kind of personal experience is persistently significant as a source for Brontë's novel. The scene of shared reading is a plain, literal report of Brontë's decades-long experience of living in Haworth, reading, and talking about reading with her sisters and brother, as well as with her father and her aunt Branwell. And there was an unusual dimension to her experience of literature. While the family could share in the reading of contemporary writers like Scott and William Wordsworth, as well as classic writers like Shakespeare and Milton, they were also, uniquely, reading the works family members were writing. Her father, Patrick, had been publishing books of poetry and prose narratives from his early days as a young Cambridge graduate and continued to contribute letters to local papers on issues of the day. Charlotte had read the poems, and, when they were prepared for publication, the novels of her sisters; thus, Emily's *Wuthering Heights* and Anne's *Agnes Grey* were all very much on Brontë's mind as she worked on *Jane Eyre*, constituting worlds of imagining other than hers and of compelling importance to her. Of far greater significance, however, were the decades of writing she had shared with Branwell, which we have already seen to be at times far more "real" than her experience of daily life. Their co-created, darkly satanic Zamorna, the beautiful and vulnerable Mary Percy, the lavish and hedonistic life of Verdopolis, constituted a secret and powerful other world for her that existed simultaneously with daily life.

A more ordinary record of true events and experiences, a more "realistic" narrative, emerges from the quite voluminous correspondence that Brontë carried on with her close friends Ellen Nussey and Mary Taylor. In Margaret Smith's brilliant edition of her letters, we find writings that reveal Charlotte's complex personality as they chronicle innumerable details of her daily life, her relationships with others, and her anger, hope, and dreams. Again and again, what the letters detail—daily chores, the weather, complaints about family members, the arrival of strange men, plans for visits to friends, feelings of frustration, fear of aging, questions about self-worth—are a reality that the novel takes up and transforms into fiction, Charlotte Brontë becoming Jane Eyre.

What Brontë had experienced, remembered, labored over in her mind and in her emotion-laden interpretation of its significance is then joined, as she wrote *Jane Eyre* by those "bright pictures" extrapolated from the past as the basis for imagining things that never happened but that she longed for. From this process emerges scenes in which Jane is able to rescue relationships with lost family members, enjoy swift and easy success in school, triumph vindictively over women who had become her enemies, quickly win over her young pupil into an amiable docility when she was a governess, be discovered by a strangely attractive man who falls passionately in love with her, be surprised by the sudden announcement that she has inherited wealth from a forgotten relative, and, in the end, enjoy marriage, prosperity, and independence on her own terms. One of the novel's pleasing surprises is its skill in persuading readers that each of these imagined, hoped-for ends—which were never a part of Charlotte Brontë's actual life—can be plausibly achieved.

❧

Brontë wrote *Jane Eyre* virtually in secret. There is absolutely no reference to her months of work on this project in her letters to friends; indeed, there isn't the slightest suggestion that she is writing anything at all. There is no record of her telling her former co-writer

Branwell about it. She surprised her father Patrick with news about the book only *after* it had been published and had received positive reviews. Indeed, it is reasonable to wonder how much her sisters knew of what she was doing. However, her friend and first biographer Elizabeth Gaskell wrote as if certain that at Haworth during their habitual nine o'clock evening exercise with its "steady pacing up and down the sitting room" Charlotte did talk with Emily and Anne as she was writing the novel, insisting "that the remarks [they made] had seldom any effect in inducing her to alter her work, so possessed was she with the feeling that she had described reality." There couldn't be a more curious and suggestive assertion than this one. What can Charlotte have meant by the term "reality," given that the novel tells of a string of events she never experienced? That they struck her, nevertheless, as essentially a version of "reality" crucially suggests she was sure she had successfully responded to Lewes' earlier critical concern and that her book achieved the effect of "Nature and Truth" that she had sought.

When and how did she write? Some biographers believe Brontë wrote a substantial portion of the novel while in Manchester with her father, and others question how much she could have done there. Charlotte left no details.

It would seem to make sense that once back home in Haworth she was able to concentrate on her writing. And yet her days there were from the first crowded with other, pressing demands on her attention. Charlotte wrote in the midst of a small, family home where it may have been difficult to be alone. She had to care for a convalescent and demanding father; to complete her usual, assigned household chores; to negotiate with two very different and strong-willed sisters, who were at times obsessively absorbed in their own writing; and to worry about a brother who was during this same period living much of the time in the nearby town of Halifax running up bar tabs at the local pub and progressively sinking more deeply into the alcoholism that would soon kill him. Indeed, while still in Manchester, she anticipated in a letter to a friend what this life would be like: "unhappily home is not now a place of complete rest," she wrote; rather, it had become haunted by two phantoms, "Sin and Suffering . . ."

There was one brief span of time, when she reached the scenes at Thornfield that "she could not stop . . . writing incessantly for three weeks; by which time she had carried her heroine away from Thornfield, and was herself in a fever which compelled her to pause." These scenes released powerful emotions so long pent-up that they consumed her. At other points in writing *Jane Eyre* she recalled, "Sometimes weeks or even months elapsed before she felt that she had anything to add to that portion of her story which was already written." Then, she had to rely upon the revelatory action of the unconscious in sleep and dreams to release further developments in the narrative. And so, "some morning she would waken up, and the progress of her tale lay clear and bright before her, in distinct vision . . ." and she could write down "incidents and consequent thoughts, which were, in fact, more present to her mind at such times than her actual life itself." Again, that assertion: more real than life.

Because Charlotte Brontë was painfully short-sighted, she wrote her first drafts on small squares of paper that she held close to her face supported on the back of a board about the size of a book cover. Later she would copy what she had written onto letter paper. Only the final draft sent to her publishers in August of 1847 survives now. We have no outlines, notes about characters, drafts scribbled over with revisions and additions—all the sorts of fascinating first starts that many writers leave behind for us to pore over and to wonder at. Brontë's need for secrecy seems to have driven her to destroy everything about the making of the book.

When did she finish it? On March 16, 1847, she began making a fair copy of earlier parts of the novel. On the final page—as had been, since childhood, her compulsory practice on completing a text—she pens a date. This time it is 19 August 1847. She sent the manuscript to Smith, Elder, who had expressed a tentative interest, on the 24th. This manuscript in three, morocco-bound volumes, which features only minor alterations of punctuation and infrequent changes in wording, is now one of the treasures of the British Library in London. Notably, Brontë refused any suggestion that she revise a word of it, writing to Smith, Elder, "were I to retrench, to alter and to add now when I am uninterested and cold, I know I should only further injure what may be already defective."

Because of Charlotte's characteristic secrecy there is no way of knowing the sequence of the composition of *Jane Eyre*. Did she begin with the first chapter, and end with the last? Her few, elliptical comments to Elizabeth Gaskell constitute all she was later to say about the making of the novel. They suggest she wrote the book in the sequence that we now have, opening with the ten-year-old Jane in an enraged fight with her cousin John Reed and concluding with her serene marriage to Mr. Rochester a little more than ten years later. Given this probable way in which the book was written, we can begin, in Chapter Two, to discern how Brontë learned to interweave "Truth" and "Imagination" as she progressed.

2

The Red-Room

Manchester, England. August 25, 1846. Charlotte is living in rented rooms on 83 Mount Pleasant, Boundary Street, Oxford Road. Accustomed to the fresh air, isolation, and freedom of the family's Haworth parsonage perched on a hilltop, she finds herself in a wholly different world. Hot weather. "Feelings of strangeness" in this unfamiliar "big town." Outside only "those grey, weary, uniform streets where all faces" were "untouched with sunlight to her." Acute pain from a toothache that had dogged her since her arrival kept her up at night. The "abominable" smell of coal gas making her feel sick "ten times a day."

Her father's eye operation has been a success. Now, he is to be confined in a dark room for weeks to come, and Charlotte wearily realizes the time spent waiting to see if he recovers will be "dreary." He is "a prisoner in his darkened room," and so is she in an adjoining sitting room. This very day, she has received by mail the manuscript of her first novel, *The Professor*, accompanied by a publisher's brief, curt note of rejection.

At this moment, in this place, Brontë picks up her pen and writes, "There was no possibility of taking a walk that day."

These words begin Jane Eyre's "Autobiography," but they spring from this immediate moment in Brontë's life. Trapped, she begins to spin an imagined tale that will permit her to escape. Here, at the very beginning of the novel, we watch the transformation. The rest of the paragraph depicts not the industrial midlands city of Manchester but a leafless garden, winter winds, somber clouds, and penetrating rain. Rural Yorkshire weather. The world of Brontë's childhood. Though dark and cold, it's somehow liberating. Charlotte is becoming Jane.

Jane goes on, in the next sentences, to recall dreadful long walks on chilly afternoons, fingers and toes nipped by cold, heart saddened by a nurse's chiding, her sense of physical inferiority in contrast to her abusive and self-centered cousins. An adopted orphan, keenly aware of how different she is from them, Jane Eyre has been excluded from the family, "a heterogeneous thing." Living in a "very beautiful house" where, she is told, she has no right to live. Solitary, endangered, independent, the Jane Eyre of these first pages reflects many of Charlotte Brontë's most painful memories of the past—of the eight-year-old child, the youngest pupil in the Cowan Bridge School roughly bullied by the bigger girls; of the twenty-three-year-old governess made to feel inferior and insignificant in the pleasant home of a newly rich bourgeois family where she is expected to do mending and keep still; of the twenty-five-year-old English woman at a school in Brussels for girls learning French and feeling that "the difference in Country & religion makes a broad line of demarcation between us & all the rest." Indeed the germ for the novel's first paragraphs is

Charlotte's experience of unhappiness when she found herself trapped in situations where authoritarian and cruel older women tried to dominate her, and when in rebellion she opposed them: the abusive teachers at Cowan Bridge, the bossy Mrs. Chiswick of Stonegappe; and, particularly, the aloof and commanding Mme. Heger in Brussels. Charlotte's rebellious spirit, emerging on the first pages of Jane Eyre's narration, is at one with a nineteenth century spurred on by revolution and romanticism to celebrate tough individualism in a voice inspired by Byron and Scott.

As the story begins, Jane has already begun her rebellion by trying to establish a separate place of her own. Excluded from the warm fireside of the Reed family, Jane has created a refuge behind the scarlet curtains. She is seated next to a window that looks out onto "a scene of wet lawn and storm-beat shrub" a reflection of Jane's inner life. The storm mirrors her internal rage at the Reeds and her resistance to their cruel treatment. With a book in hand, for the moment she can be alone. Alone, as Brontë is while she writes these pages, and so escaping from Manchester's heat and smells, and the anxiety she feels for her father. This kind of moment was very familiar to Brontë. Many times in her life imagination had liberated her from similarly entrapping experiences. For example, ten years earlier, in 1835–1836, when she was nineteen to twenty years old, Charlotte worked as a teacher at the Roe Head school to help support her family. It was run by her generous-hearted former teacher Miss Wooler. Charlotte intensely disliked her work there, which she called "wretched bondage," writing of her pupils "if those Girls knew how I loath their company they would not seek mine." During precious and rare moments of escape from fellow teachers and students, just as Jane Eyre on a cold afternoon has escaped from the Reed family, so Charlotte would begin to free her imagination, writing extraordinary dream-like texts—a series of fragments that are now sometimes called "The Roe Head Journal."

Typical of her notes is an entry for February 4, 1836: "Last night, I did indeed lean upon the thunder-wakening wings of such a stormy blast . . . and it whirled me away like heath in the wilderness for five seconds of ecstasy." Separated from the others, Brontë enters a rapturous trance, returning to the world that she and her brother Branwell had been imagining and writing about for years. It has for her a far more powerful emotional content than her daily experiences. The word "ecstasy" is not casually chosen. It reveals the strong sexual component of these private and secret reveries.

Another time she describes a similar plunge into fantasy—quoted here at length as our first glimpse into the world of Angria:

> Never shall I, Charlotte Brontë, forget what a voice of wild and wailing music now came thrillingly to my mind's—almost my body's—ear; nor how distinctly I, sitting in the schoolroom at Roe Head, saw the Duke of Zamorna leaning against that obelisk, . . . the moonlight so mild and so exquisitely tranquil, sleeping upon that vast and vacant road, and the African sky quivering and shaking with stars expanded above all. I was quite gone. I had really utterly forgot where I was and all the gloom and cheerlessness of my situation. I felt myself breathing quick and short as I beheld the Duke lifting up his sable crest . . . and knew that that music . . . was exciting him and quickening his ever rapid pulse.

In this utterly fictional Africa—immensely expansive yet tranquil—Charlotte sees her favorite character, the dark and immoral Zamorna, experiencing excitement in the music that she intimately shares. It is a strangely erotic moment. Insistently identifying herself—note how frequently "I" appears in this passage—Charlotte lives another life. Every element of this fantasy scene, later on, enters into *Jane Eyre*. The novel liberates her from the anxieties and unhappiness of home and her sexual longing.

Aware of the danger and the power of these experiences, Charlotte writes in a letter of May 1836 from Roe Head to her close friend Ellen Nussey, "If you knew my thoughts; the dreams that absorb me; the fiery imagination that at times eats me up . . . you would pity and I dare say despise me." While Charlotte admits the depths to which her imagination takes her, she also believes that her imagination's unruliness is inappropriate for a young woman.

In the first pages of the novel, then, Jane Eyre has, just like Brontë, created for herself a secret place where her imagination can run free. Jane has a book—a copy of which was in Charlotte Brontë's father's library—the popular and much admired *History of British Birds* illustrated with wood engravings by Thomas Bewick.

This book is crucial in many ways. Think only of Fairfax Rochester's later description of Jane Eyre as a "wild, frantic bird." Bewick's art is essential to Brontë's descriptions—crucial to the emotional core of her novel. Its depictions of the solitary birds of the northern seas become, as we are about to see, key to Jane Eyre's understanding of herself. Hence, as she picks it from the shelf, Bewick both takes this ten-year-old child away from the present, unhappy moment and yet forces her to look inward into who she is and what is happening to her.

When Charlotte began *Jane Eyre*, Bewick and his birds had already played an important and unusual role in her inner life. In 1829 she had copied two of its pictures (when she was twelve and thirteen), "Cormorant on rocky coast" and "Fisherman sheltering against a tree"—the first, a single bird on wave-battered rocks; the second, a fisherman in a driving rain huddled next to a thick, aged tree trunk, a large mansion in the distance. Both pictures are filled with elements that will appear in her novel seventeen years later: cold, solitary figures in a hostile world of swirling wind and rain. Why did young Charlotte choose these two images for her typically deliberate and minute copying? She must have sensed that they represented an aspect of her inner plight that, further, anticipates the inner life of her future heroine—a defiant loneliness in a world which could sometimes seem full of cold indifference.

A couple of years later, on learning of Bewick's death, the sixteen-year-old Charlotte wrote a poem celebrating his genius. To her, his art is remarkably "True to the common Nature that we see / In England's sunny fields, her hills, and vales," but also true to other nature scenes, such as "the wild bosom of her storm-dark sea / Still heaving to the wind that o'er it wails." In these lines she marks the diversity of his work. Bewick was both a romantic and a realist. His book—essentially a catalogue of birds seen in Britain— offers individual entries for each species, depicted in half-page wood cuts with scientifically accurate details. But when an entry finishes before the end of a page, Bewick then includes "tailpieces," decorative pictures of the England he knew. Living in Newcastle on Tyne, and loving the countryside, Bewick often depicts dense woods, lush undergrowth, and gently meandering streams. We see hunters and fishermen, and also local people, many of them working class, and even some impoverished beggars: a world very different from the barren, rolling moors beyond Haworth that had been Brontë's landscape, and which may have made them attractive to her as a consequence. At other times Bewick turns to hilly, even mountainous landscapes, long roads winding toward distant villages, wanderers with bundles on their backs—far more a world Brontë knew. Far more like later scenes in *Jane Eyre* when, fleeing Mr. Rochester, Jane trudges solitary in dismal weather through the moors near death.

Charlotte's poem moves on to celebrate her youthful experiences of *British Birds*, reading the text, closely scrutinizing the engravings, and how it stirred her visual imagination. "Our childhood's days return, again in thought / We wander in a land of love and light . . . Sweet flowers seem gleaming 'mid the tangled grass / Sparkling with spring-drops from the rushing rill." Charlotte admires Bewick's more remote images as well, which have their grounding in his second volume with its sea birds and tailpieces frequently depicting people on the shore, rocky cliffs, and ships at sea. They are more like the later scenes in *Jane Eyre*: "There rises some lone rock, all wet with surge / And dashing billows glimmering in the light / Of a wan moon whose silent rays emerge / From clouds that veil their lustre cold and bright."

The poem's narrator continues to turn the pages admitting, "I cannot speak the rapture that I feel / When on the work of such a mind I gaze." The modern reader may find a similar experience in paging through Bewick, the rich variety of his scenes, his sensitivity to ordinary life—not only men plowing fields, women hanging out wash, but also a slightly desperate traveler urinating on a ruined wall, a wanderer fending off snapping guard dogs, a peg-legged beggar resting, an old man and a boy scrutinizing inscriptions on an ancient isolated pillar.

And so when Charlotte has Jane Eyre pull down "a volume, taking care that it should be one stored with pictures," Charlotte seizes upon a book that is one of her favorites. She has it speak powerfully but secretively to Jane, who opens the second volume and, closely echoing Bewick's text, finds herself drawn to his description "of the haunts of sea-fowl; of 'the solitary rock and promontories' by them only inhabited"—which is to say, her world. "Of these death-white realms I formed an idea of my own: shadowy, like all the half-comprehended notions that float dim through children's brains, but strangely impressive." In a brilliant narrative move, Brontë brings the reader into the most private and remote parts of Jane's inner life. Jane, like Charlotte the unhappy school teacher at Roe Head, has escaped into a world of imagination. There, free from the social and economic humiliations imposed on her by the Reed family, she can enter "a story; mysterious often to my undeveloped understanding and imperfect feelings, yet ever profoundly interesting." Jane scans and interprets these pictures much as Charlotte had. Close school friend Mary Taylor later recalled the short-sighted Brontë: "Whenever an opportunity offered of examining a picture or a cut of any kind, she went over it piecemeal, with her eyes close to the paper, looking so long that we used to ask her 'What she saw in it.' She could always see plenty, and explained it very well."

So important are these pictures to Charlotte as well as to Jane, that Jane lists seven of them. Most can be quickly found on Bewick's pages. All are desolate, such as a rock "standing up alone" in a sea of billow and spray—there are at least three versions of this scene in Bewick—others are depictions of tragedy seen at a remote distance, such as the moon breaking through clouds illuminating a sinking wreck, where a terrifying wall of rock shelves out, snow covered, into a stormy sea. More tranquil but no less ominous is a solitary church-yard with its inscribed headstone; its low horizon, girdled by a broken wall, and its "newly-risen crescent, attesting the hour of eventide."

Jane omits the ominous inscription on that headstone, "Good Times / & / Bad Times / & / All Times / get over," but the fearful sense of death's menace is present in her description.

As the list continues, Jane's attention becomes attracted by two further images. Both come from the first volume of *British Birds*. These fearfully move on from the realistic to the supernatural. In the first a full moon hovers over a distant gate. In the foreground a man hauls a large, heavy sack by a strap pulled over his shoulders. The sack, tied at the top, is large enough to hold a dead body. Jane and Brontë name him a thief, but nothing in the picture demands this interpretation. Behind the man a black figure, much smaller than a man, with a pointed tail, bat wings, and horns springing from its head, jams a stick through the base of the pack and into a rock outcropping thus pinning it down. What this might mean is a matter of subjective inference. And that's the point. Simple moralizing might read it as a depiction of guilt and punishment. The moonlit sky, the distant gate, the entrapment suggest a burden tied up in that sack, which the man struggles to carry while the demon holds him down with reckless glee. The very indeterminacy demands speculation that carries the viewer into unexpected reveries. Could this be a nightmare version of Jane's feelings of entrapment? Of the burden of her difference?

The second of the two, a tiny image, depicts the same sort of gleeful fiend perched on a rock and to the left far in the distance a crowd of dark figures surrounding a gallows on which a dead man hangs. Death by hanging seems to have fascinated Bewick. Among his woodcuts are pictures of suicide by hanging, execution by hanging, even cruel people hanging dogs. For Brontë and for Jane these pictures open up a world of terror, the fearful actions of people, and the immanence of the diabolical.

These images possess a kind of magnetic attraction precisely because they are so horrifying. Jane cannot stop looking at them. They are not so much an escape from her present moment as a presentation and a confirmation of who she is and what she faces. She too is the solitary cormorant, the wrecked ship; she too struggles with that strange weight on her back as she staggers toward the moonlit gate. For the first chapter of *Jane Eyre* they constitute an apt prologue for the events to follow. Further, Jane's obsessive curiosity about the uncanny in Bewick proves a remarkable presentment for her future terrors in the midnight darkened rooms of Thornfield.

However, Jane, just like the youthful Charlotte, isn't lost for very long in her dreamy, gothic fantasies. There is an abrupt and brutal interruption.

At Roe Head, Brontë's written reverie quoted above is interrupted. Reality, in the form of one of the school's pupils, breaks in: "'Miss Brontë, what are you thinking about?' said a voice that dissipated all the charm, and Miss [Harriet] Lister thrust her little, rough black head into my face!" Charlotte's effort at escape through fantasy images of Zamorna ends with comic irony. In just the same way, on another evening, as she is picturing Quashia, an enemy of Zamorna, a savage powerfully attractive with "his tusk-like teeth glancing vindictively through his parted lips . . . the dining-room door opened and Miss W[ooler] came in with a plate of butter in her hand. 'A very stormy night my dear!' said she: 'it is ma'm' said I." Shattering Jane's reverie and her personal haven.

Jane Eyre's reverie isn't interrupted by curious or kind people. Rather, it is John Reed, her fourteen-year-old cousin, a boy of "dingy and unwholesome skin," "thick lineaments," and "heavy limbs." This

obnoxious lad comes from two earlier Brontë novels, one by Charlotte, one by her sister Anne, completed in the months before the
composition of *Jane Eyre*. Charlotte's *The Professor*, based on her experiences in Brussels, characterizes Belgian boys with "intellectual faculties [that] were generally weak, [but] their animal propensities strong."
Indeed, their natures were "dull, but they were also singularly stub-
born, heavy as lead . . . having short memories, dense intelligence,
feeble reflective power . . . " John Reed also emerged from Anne
Brontë's first novel, *Agnes Grey*. When only a little more than eighteen
years old, Anne served for nine months (April–December 1839) as
governess for the Ingham family of Blake Hall, Mirfield, in charge of
the two oldest children. In her novel based on this experience, Agnes'
new pupil Tom Bloomfield introduces himself by showing her his
trapped birds, boasting "sometimes I cut them in pieces with my pen-
knife; but the next, I mean to roast alive." Completely undisciplined,
Tom and his sisters Mary Ann and Fanny run wild behind the house
where "they seemed to prefer the dirtiest places, and the most dismal
occupations." Tom refuses "to learn or repeat his lessons," and when
compelled stands "twisting his body and his face into the most grotesque and singular contortions." Tom's stupidity and cruelty become
John Reed's constant bullying of Jane Eyre, to the point where "every
morsel of flesh on my bones shrank when he came near." Reed exults
over Jane's social and economic inferiority and gloats over his posses-
sion, as the eldest male in the family, of the book in her hand. He
snatches the copy of Bewick from Jane and in a kind of ritualized
punishment forces her to stand "out of the way of the mirrors and
window" so he can throw it at her face. Jane falls, cutting her head.

Charlotte spoke of a similar experience. As a twenty-three-year-
old governess working for the Sidgwick family, she was caring for
one of the younger Sidgwick sons when the child's older brother

"tempted the little fellow into the forbidden place." Charlotte followed and tried to persuade the younger boy to come away; but, instigated by his brother, he threw stones at her, and one of them hit her "so severe a blow on the temple that the lads were alarmed into obedience." Throwing things at the governess seems to have been a bit of a Sidgwick habit. Earlier, a cousin threw a Bible at her.

For Jane, John Reed's throwing Bewick at her head has powerful symbolic resonance since this fourteen-year-old boy clearly doesn't respect books at all while Bewick has just been a portal into the refuge of her imagination. Since her childhood Charlotte had been a writer of tiny, handmade books. She came from a family where books were not merely objects to possess but rather treasured emblems of learning and worth. In the library at Haworth, Charlotte had seen volumes Patrick Brontë had won at Cambridge when he was a student, special copies of Horace and Homer later bound in leather with the college arms on the covers and inside his own inscriptions such as, in the *Iliad,* "'My Prize Book, for having always kept in the <u>first class</u>, at St John's College—Cambridge." Patrick instilled in his children the significance and value of books that John Reed defiles.

The moment recapitulates in striking ways the earlier scene with the Sidgwick boy. Both depict a brutal male effort at dominance over an unjustly subordinated woman. To get along, Charlotte as governess decided not to report the event. She even fibbed the next day when at lunch she was asked about the bruise on her head. But when she wrote *Jane Eyre* her heroine was not so pliant.

During the ensuing scuffle, Jane attacks her bigger and stronger male cousin with such frenzy that she no longer recalls, writing some thirty years later, what she did with her hands, but it shocks the maids who come to part them: "What a fury" one of them exclaims, alluding to a particularly fearsome Greek demon we will return to in Chapter Eight when we consider parallels between Jane Eyre and Mr. Rochester's wife, Bertha.

Mrs. Reed arrives, barking out a peremptory order that again anticipates Bertha's fate: she orders Jane locked up in a room. Mrs. Reed comes, as we have seen, from a gallery of powerful female opponents in Charlotte's life. Jane's rebellion on this darkening afternoon is the first, dramatic release of her "ire"—a term that serves to alert the reader at the beginning of the novel that her name echoes not only "eyrie," which means the nest of a large bird, especially a bird of prey, but also the involuntary rage that sometimes overwhelms Jane as a form of liberation, which in a later scene seems to so alarm Mrs. Reed that she is unsure whether Jane is "child or fiend." Now, like a "mad cat," she is dragged into the room in which her former patron, the kindly Mr. Reed, died, the servants threatening to tie her down in a chair until she acquiesces to her imprisonment. This is a profoundly autobiographical moment for Brontë. As we will now see, it condenses a range and variety of her past, giving a sudden glimpse into her inner life.

As Jane's rage dwindles, she finds settling over her, her "habitual mood of humiliation, self-doubt, forlorn depression . . ." For the novel's author, this is a particularly important autobiographical echo. Brontë was also prone to periods of intense despondency. In 1838, while still teaching in Miss Wooler's school, she recalled, "My health and spirits had utterly failed me." She described this crisis moment years later—significantly during the months when she was drafting *Jane Eyre*—as an anxious time when she felt a "most dreadful doom . . . far worse than that of a man with healthy nerves buried for the same length of time in a subterranean dungeon." This nightmare imprisonment, being buried alive, was a crucial narrative element in the gothic fiction Brontë loved as a young reader. But now overwhelmed by depression in the late 1830s, she experiences a particular form of "anguish" that she considered even worse than this terrifying fate, during which a "preternatural horror . . . seemed to clothe existence," making her life a nightmare. A time when "the morbid Nerves can know neither peace nor enjoyment—whatever touches—pierces them—sensation for them is all suffering." Brontë didn't need to read works such as Edgar Allan Poe's "The Fall of the House of Usher" (1839) with Roderick's exquisitely painful hypersensitivity alert to the desperate cries of his sister Madeline—buried alive beneath their house. The crucial elements of this description in Brontë's letter all derive from earlier gothic fiction.

The fourteen-year-old Charlotte had anticipated these motifs in her 1830 tale titled "An Extraordinary Dream." There the narrator, Charles Wellesley, overcome by the chills and burning fever of a strange illness finds himself suddenly unable to move or speak even though his senses remain keen. He watches as his family members weep over his rigid body, then cover it with a white sheet. Fears of "being buried with dead bodies amid stench and putrefaction" consume him as he is put into a "leaden coffin . . . the nails . . . screwed down," and he is lowered into the family vault. "By degrees the sound of the multitude died away and not a voice or step echoed through the vast aisles which but to think of is unsupportable agony." In 1836, while she was teaching at Roe Head, separated from her coauthor Branwell and unable to achieve any sustained writing, Charlotte must have felt buried alive in the remote school for girls. She speculated whether her brother, who was continuing to write

back at Haworth, had killed off her favorite heroine Mary Percy, "Is
she dead, is she buried is she alone in the cold earth . . . under the
bleak pavement of a church in a vault closed up with lime mortar."
This provokes a series of "wretched thoughts." "I hope she's alive,"
Brontë continues, "because I can't abide to think how hopelessly &
cheerlessly she must have died." These experiences are analogous to
how she feels when she describes her depression of 1838; although
Charlotte asserts it's even worse to be living what seems an ordinary
life surrounded and closed in by a sensation where everything is as
horrifying as a nightmare.

Jane Eyre in the locked, darkening red-room, suddenly terrified
that Mr. Reed's spirit might appear in the house, relives Charlotte's
feelings of psychological entrapment and anguish. During the profound despondency of 1838, as Brontë later recalled later to Elizabeth
Gaskell, "She could not forget the gloom, could not sleep at night, nor
attend in the day" and "that one night sitting alone . . . she heard a
voice repeat" lines of poetry that she had never written. Her father,
recuperating in Manchester while she writes, is also a "prisoner in his
darkened room," awaiting anxiously the medical verdict about his
eyesight and whether he can keep his employment. All are trapped,
just like Jane. The prisoner in the darkened room is a version of the
man buried alive in a subterranean dungeon and the child in the red-
room of ire, blood, and fire, threatened with supernatural visitations.

This shrouded world was nothing new for Brontë. Living at the
edge of an early Victorian industrial town, with all the consequent
health problems and short life spans for many people, death and
dying were always close by. Consider, for example, the wet and rainy
winter of 1833–1834 when Charlotte was seventeen. At Haworth
there was "an unusual number of deaths in the village . . . the passing and funeral bells so frequently tolling, filling the heavy air with

their mournful sound—and . . . the 'chip, chip' of the mason, as he cut the grave stones in a shed close by." Visitors to the rectory at Haworth are usually struck immediately by the fact that its windows look out upon a graveyard, the sight of which greeted the Brontë children every morning. While today that place is shadowed by aged trees, when they lived there, there were no trees and the tombstones stood raw and isolated in an otherwise bare space. Charlotte told of seeing from her bedroom window "no other landscape than a monotonous stretch of moorland, a grey church tower, rising from the centre of a church-yard so filled with graves, that rank-weed and coarse grass scarce had room to shoot up between the monuments." Inside that parish church was the funerary monument to the memory of her mother and two older sisters near to which Charlotte and her siblings would have sat and prayed. Writing from Haworth in March of 1845, a year and a half before beginning the writing of *Jane Eyre,* Charlotte says, "There was a time when Haworth was a very pleasant place to me; it is not so now—I feel as if we were all buried here."

Brontë's use of Bewick's engravings evokes the dark side of living in Haworth: the dismal churchyard out her childhood window, the deaths of family and friends both long ago and recent. In ways easy to understand, the shared, fearful fascination of both the writer and her character regarding death and the spectral return of the dead expresses their conflicted longing for those who died. Jane locked in the red-room terrified at the possibility of the appearance of the guilt-filled uncle seems both a natural fear of the dead mixed with a desire for him to return and avenge his wife's bad treatment of her.

Indeed the return of the vengeful dead, intent upon punishing injustice in the world of the living, had a particular attraction to Charlotte. In her poem "Gilbert"—written only months before she began *Jane Eyre*—we find a similar kind of action played out. Charlotte's poem depicts the central character Gilbert recalling a sadistic relationship with a woman named Elinor and the days when he enjoyed watching her "kneel, / In bondage, at my feet." Much as John Reed enjoyed Jane's fall and wounding, Gilbert relished witnessing Elinor's anguish and pain, but, then, he discards her. In despair she drowns herself. Years later, when he is prosperous, married, and supposedly secure, her specter haunts him. In the climactic, final scene, Gilbert comes home at midnight. The moon is out, and rain is in the air. At his door he knocks three times. The door opens to reveal "A woman, clad in white. / Lo! Water from her dripping dress / Runs on the streaming floor; / From every dark and clinging tress, / The drops incessant pour." He attempts to brush past the specter, but she drifts ahead of him. He falls to his knees praying, but she will not move. Wildly, as if possessed by demons, he rushes up the staircase and into his room. He seizes a knife and cuts his throat. Through the gash "his outraged life / Rushed rash and redly through." Elinor's revenge on Gilbert is similar to the one that Jane wishes Mr. Reed would inflict upon his son and wife, the scarlet flow of his blood anticipating the drapery that conceals the young Jane in Chapter One, and the "deep red damask" that festoons the dead man's bed in Chapter Two. At the same time, she imagines Mr. Reed as a fearful thing that she cannot control. Jane has become frightened that her rage and vengefulness might be turned against her. She looked in the mirror and saw a "tiny phantom" reflected back; the darkness and her fear push her to the brink of madness. Unaware of what she is doing, Jane cries out. The servants say, "What a scream" as they enter. Brontë transposes the darkness of her world into the literal and terrifying darkness of Jane's in the red-room.

For Charlotte Brontë and for Jane Eyre much of their secret lives are lived on the borderline of madness, and there are moments of anguish when its darkness takes over. Jane will find that the Jamaican planter and merchant's daughter Bertha Mason has succumbed to its allure and now lives in her own version of the red-room, a locked cell on the third floor of Thornfield Hall, little more than a pitiful, savage beast.

And then come consolations. The first, in the form of a quite different man than the ghost of the vengeful dead: the local apothecary Mr. Lloyd. His tender care and willingness to hear what Jane has to say makes her feel "sheltered and befriended." He anticipates Mr. Rochester in his kinder moods. The second, and ultimately far more important, is the servant Bessie, offering Jane a tart on her favorite plate, decorated with a brightly feathered "bird of paradise." She keeps Jane, whose nerves are shattered, company. Bessie is a kind of threshold figure. At Jane's request she brings her a copy of *Gulliver's Travels* and sings of "the path of the poor orphan child." As such she has a kind of double function recalling Charlotte's sisterhood with Emily and Anne: she nurtures, shares in a caring telling of story and song such as Charlotte loved in her life at Haworth, but at the same time recurrently seems to suggest that soon Jane, like Charlotte, will necessarily start on a journey that will challenge her.

Indeed, Jane must leave, "severed from Bessie and Gateshead: thus whirled away to unknown, . . . remote and mysterious regions."

And so Jane embarks upon the "road of trials," one of the earliest and most important story forms in European literature. Think: Homer, Virgil, Dante, Swift, Defoe. The traditional protagonist is a man—wily like Odysseus, self-disciplined like Aeneas, foolish like Robinson Crusoe, confused like Gulliver, divinely led like Dante.

As he pursues his journey toward a distant goal—often enough it's simply returning home—he meets challenges that threaten him. Each is a test.

It's an aspect of Brontë's genius that while working in this literary tradition she chooses to write about a young girl. Jane encounters the unexpected and the terrifying, just like those ancient heroes, facing whatever threatens her, choosing for herself, and never giving up.

3

Injustice

A s she planned out the novel, Brontë necessarily sought to
invent for her heroine a challenging next step in her road of
trials. Looking back upon her own experience she found
nothing quite as suitable, which is to say painful and devastating,
as her year-long enrollment in the Clergy Daughters School at
Cowan Bridge. This school, just opened, was a charitable concern
intended to help poorly paid Church of England priests with their
daughters' education. With his wife Maria now dead, this must
have seemed to Patrick Brontë an unexpected boon. He sent to the
school his four oldest: Maria, Elizabeth, Charlotte, and Emily. He
couldn't have known much about the place when he sent them.
Their treatment there was so horrendous that the next spring Maria
and Elizabeth returned home to die, while Charlotte was physically and emotionally damaged for life.

Thus in framing the chapters that follow Jane's departure from
Gateshead, Brontë chose to write about Cowan Bridge for two dis-

tinct reasons. First, it would offer scenes of high drama as Jane faces new challenges that help forge her spirit. Second, it would offer Brontë the chance to indict the school and those who ran it. Helen Burns, Jane's first and best friend at the school, is later to speak in surprise of Jane Eyre's indignation at Mrs. Reed: "What a singularly deep impression her injustice seems to have made on your heart!" The same is true for Charlotte—she too seeks to attack past injustice and to do it in Jane's way: to tell "the *truth*." Few things could be more personally meaningful to Brontë than this.

Mrs. Reed wants to be rid of Jane. The child has no choice in what happens. And Mrs. Reed has a plan. In a scene enacted in Jane's presence, she calls in a clergyman named Brocklehurst who runs a charitable school for orphans named Lowood Institution. She stages it in the breakfast room, the site for Jane's earlier violent confrontation with John Reed. In doing this she dramatically illustrates that this will be her final vindication and triumph over this rebellious ten-year-old girl. Mrs. Reed explains that she wants Jane to have an education "suiting her prospects," by which she means little money and no hopes for the future. Mrs. Reed wants Jane to be made useful and humble. Brocklehurst questions Jane's past conduct, asking if she will "repent of ever having been the occasion of discomfort to your excellent benefactress." The terms are clear from the outset. Jane is beholden to Mrs. Reed. Lurking behind this interrogation is the Reeds' imprisonment of Jane in the red-room. Mrs. Reed wants to stifle any of Jane's protestations in advance. She instructs Brocklehurst that "the superintendent and teachers [of Lowood school should] . . . keep a strict eye on her, and above all, to guard against her worst fault, a tendency to deceit." She is trying to prevent Jane from telling others what happened on that day. His reply is to use the false, pseudo-biblical rhetoric to which he always resorts: "all liars will have their portion in the lake burning with fire and brimstone." Before he leaves, he hands Jane a pamphlet, telling her, "here is a book entitled the 'Child's Guide'; read it with prayer, especially that part containing 'an account of the awfully sudden death of Martha G—, a naughty child addicted to falsehood and deceit.'"

Brocklehurst is an exact copy of the clergyman Charlotte had to face at Cowan Bridge, the Rev. William Carus Wilson. Wilson wrote similar pamphlets that reveled in the gruesome thought of children dying young and which threatened their child-readers with divine punishment for what most people would regard as minor faults. For example, his *Child's First Tales* (1836) features a story "Child in a pet" about a young girl who "would have her own way. Oh! How cross she looks. And oh! What a sad tale have I to tell you of her. She was in such a rage, that all at once God struck her dead . . . And oh! Where do you think she is now? . . . We know that bad girls go to hell when they die." Remembering Wilson and his cruel hypocrisy, Charlotte now sends her heroine to be under his tutelage and control. In so doing, she now will tell readers the truth about her past.

⤙⤚

Charlotte Brontë was enrolled in the Clergy Daughter's School at Cowan Bridge on August 10, 1824, when she was a little over eight years old. Jane Eyre arrives at the Lowood Institution on the January 19 when she is ten. Brontë's narrative in Chapters V to IX of *Jane Eyre* are the most literally autobiographical part of the novel. Responding to a certain anxiety expressed by the editors at Smith, Elder about these chapters, Charlotte Brontë replied, "Had I told <u>all</u> the truth, I might indeed have made it far more exquisitely painful," but she preferred to avoid displeasing her more sensitive readers. While this is by no means the only part of the novel that raised questions about verisimilitude upon its first publication, it was certainly one of the central places where questions of accuracy and fairness emerged. Brontë was always insistent that her recreation of the school was factual. Her friend and first biographer Elizabeth Gaskell was later to recall, "Miss Brontë more than once said to me . . . there was not a word in her account of the institution but what was true at the time when she knew it." As we have already seen, Charlotte Brontë's insistence goes far beyond an author's pride in accuracy. Because she cared so deeply about this question of "truth," she was delighted when she saw a local clergyman reading *Jane Eyre*, and to overhear him saying " 'Why – they have got – School, and Mr. – here, I declare! And Miss – (naming the originals of Lowood, Mr. Brocklehurst and Miss Temple)' " and, adding to Charlotte's satisfaction, that Brocklehurst " 'deserved the chastisement he had got.' " There is a note of triumph in her words.

Elizabeth Gaskell's *The Life of Charlotte Brontë*, appearing two years after Charlotte's death, fueled the debate. Its discussion of the Cowan Bridge scenes characterizes them as based on "[t]he pictures, ideas, and conceptions of character received into the mind of the child of eight years old," which were "destined to be reproduced in fiery words a quarter of a century afterwards." Gaskell's account, for all its caution, almost immediately sparked a firestorm. The model for Mr. Brocklehurst, W. Carus Wilson, was still very much alive. His friends rallied around the Rev. Henry Shepheard, Wilson's son-in-law, who published *A Vindication of the Clergy Daughter's School and the Rev. W. Carus Wilson*. Stung by their angry critique, Gaskell issued two revisions of her biography, the third edition, in particular, muting some of the most critical remarks about Cowan

Bridge from the book's first edition. It should be added her initial assessments and characterizations were almost certainly correct. I will rely on them here.

The powerful and secret motives for Charlotte Brontë's "fiery words" were, first, her certainty that her two older sisters died because during the months they were at the school they were treated so badly; and, second, that she was permanently damaged both physically and psychologically. Her bad teeth, her underdeveloped body, her reticence and secretiveness, her tendency to despondency bordering at times on mania, all could, with some justification, be seen as the consequences of her time there. Brontë had become the "avenging sister of the sufferer"—that sufferer being not only her sisters but also herself.

The question of truthfulness, then, debated by Wilson's supporters, and raised elsewhere by some of the novel's earliest reviewers and critics, was an intensely personal one for Brontë—and in the novel, even before its publication and subsequent reception, she anticipated the debate in Jane Eyre's angry confrontation, after Brocklehurst's departure, with Mrs. Reed. With "ungovernable excitement" Jane Eyre insists upon the accuracy of her narrative of the red-room, affirming "I will tell anybody who asks me questions this exact tale," because it is "the *truth*."

⌘

Brontë had experienced her own road of trials. Hers began early with the death of her mother Maria on September 15, 1821. Charlotte was only five years old. Her mother's illness had been a long and painful one, and, given the relative closeness of the rooms at Haworth, the small child must have been aware of what was happening—the pain, the wasting away, the fear, the grief. Brontë was usually quiet about this first tragedy in her life. It was, however, to have an important influence on *Jane Eyre*. But immediately, for her, it meant a family home without a mother, with a father struggling to raise six small children and carry on his demanding work as a parish priest. When her father sent her off to the just-opened Cowan Bridge School for girls the shock of this second change in her life must have been overwhelming. She had grown up in a close family home. She wrote in later years of the "affection which brothers and sisters feel for each other . . . when they have clung to each other from childhood." This clinging, this family closeness, was suddenly stripped from her, as was the routine of a daily life in which eating, playing, and the rudiments of learning and self-expression took place within a quiet domestic context. Intimacy and love, freedom and respect were suddenly replaced with an institutional life of rules and the ringing of bells to denote each activity, accompanied by hunger, cold, and a radical loneliness felt in the midst of rude and indifferent strangers.

Brontë makes Jane two years older than when she went to Cowan Bridge. Jane is more experienced and tougher than she was because Jane has been hardened by the rough treatment, emotional and physical, that she had to endure in the Reed home. Everything must have been worse for Charlotte: more terrifying, more overwhelming, more meaningless. This is one of the aspects of the novel's Lowood scenes that, as she reassured her publishers, were worse in actual experience than what readers find in the book. The secret history of *Jane Eyre* is one that is at times of things too painful to send out into the world in a novel meant to be enjoyed. At the same time—just like Jane Eyre defying Mrs. Reed—Brontë as a writer insists on telling the truth. Mid-Victorian readers were appalled to learn from Elizabeth Gaskell that the school Jane had endured had been a real school and not some fiction cooked up by the superheated imagination of a writer. The indignant efforts on the part of Wilson's defenders to gloss over how bad things had been failed. A subsequent century-and-a-half of research has concluded that Brontë's account is factual. Things were that bad, indeed, worse.

What Brontë writes in *Jane Eyre* is an indictment of criminal acts, a narrative of child abuse justified by social, economic, and religious hypocrisy that she presents as an integrated "system"—a term Mrs. Reed uses in praising it. Brocklehurst, during his visit to Mrs. Reed, proclaims, "Consistency, madam, is the first of Christian duties; and it has been observed in every arrangement connected with the establishment of Lowood." This moment of candor will show Brocklehurst's consistency to be that of impoverishing the girls physically and psychologically. Brontë has this clergyman forget the first—and indeed several other—Christian duties found in the Gospels, replacing them with organizational integration and rigor. Indeed the most apt parallel to this girls school is prison. Bondage, torture, humiliation—being buried alive. It's as if the red-room has been turned into this institution.

When Jane arrives at Lowood, exhausted by a long coach ride, she is led by an under-teacher "from compartment to compartment, from passage to passage, of a large and irregular building." A dark and bewildering labyrinth, far larger than any place Jane—or Charlotte at age eight—has ever been in before; its size and complexity presents an architecture of power and domination. The forces that laid out and constructed these spaces are now enclosing and trapping the little girl moving through them. Jane hears the humming of voices and comes at last on "a wide, long room, with great deal tables, two at each end, on each of which burnt a pair of candles, and seated all around on benches a congregation of girls of every age . . ." There are more than eighty of them, "uniformly dressed in brown stuff frocks of quaint fashion, and long holland pinafores." The humming sound comes from the girls' "whispered repetitions" of the lessons they are learning. Number here is crucial. The total number of students in this very large room, its organization into numbered tables and benches, illumination by symmetrical and numbered candles illustrates how the system considers and treats the girls as undifferentiated integers. Each is simply another number. The students, a wide range of ages, are being forced into anonymity through regulated tasks and through uniform and drab clothes; they have become a hive of drones humming the essentially mindless repetition of lessons not to be considered or discussed, much less questioned, but rather simply memorized. "Silence!" and "Order!" shouts the teacher the next morning as classes begin. The students subside into "the low, vague hum of numbers," an "indefinite sound."

The sense of imprisonment comes through in the regulated schedule. The school day is, as Jane Eyre tells us, "Business," and time is defined by the sound of bells and the barked commands of the teachers. "Monitors, collect the lesson books, and put them away!" "Monitors, fetch the supper-trays!" Students are addressed by their last names. Older girls "monitor" the younger in a classic prison structure in which some prisoners are privileged to discipline the others. Rest comes in rooms with long rows of beds, two girls to each. When they awake in the chilly predawn, they wash in basins of cold water sometimes iced over by freezing temperatures.

Underlying the structure of this disciplinary system are two ruling assumptions. The first is that students are essentially unruly and undisciplined animals. This notion was widespread during the nineteenth century and given a darker implication when institutions were dominated, as Lowood was, by a Calvinistic religious ethic that stressed the wickedness deep in the hearts of children. The second, equally coercive and harmful is that the girls at Lowood are to be trained into subservience. As females they are secondary to men; as charity students they are socially inferior to others; economic realities dictate they will never have enough. The students at this institution must prepare themselves for male dominance, second-class social status, and drab moderation in all things. Their appearance dramatically symbolizes, as do the uniforms of prisoners, their interchangeability and lack of importance: "all with plain locks combed from their faces, not a curl visible; in brown dresses, made high and surrounded by a narrow tucker about the throat, with little pockets of Holland . . . tied in front of their frocks, and destined to serve the purpose of a work-bag: all too wearing woolen stockings and country-made shoes, fastened with brass buckles." All, all. The rhythm of Jane's prose chants the oppressive sameness. The biographer Winifred Gérin quotes the original Cowan Bridge prospectus which lists and describes with military precision the clothing students were required to bring. Flannel petticoats (two), white and black stockings, four brown Holland pinafores, pairs of stays, and so on. Significantly, the physical traces of female sexuality are covered over or cut off. Choked silent by the "narrow tucker about the throat," expecting little in their "little pockets," which are principally for carrying work, their dresses uniform in drab color and made of cheap, coarse cloth, their clunky shoes and woolen stockings anticipating the cold and the hard work. Everything to make them unattractive, clumsy, and sexless. All of this, on Brontë's part, is simply reporting what she had witnessed and experienced, although it evokes much.

For individuals who do not subordinate to the rules there is immediate physical discipline. There is no evidence that Charlotte had experienced or witnessed corporal punishment during her childhood at Haworth. Her father and aunt seem to have been loath to correct the Brontë children in this way. She must have been shocked to witness this kind of thing when she arrived at Cowan Bridge. Jane first sees ritual punishment given by a "little and dark" teacher named Miss Scatcherd, "smartly dressed, but of somewhat morose aspect" who has chosen to bear down on a student named Helen Burns, who has become Jane's only friend and whose importance to the whole novel will soon emerge. Scatcherd issues an order, and Burns gets a bundle of twigs that she hands to the teacher "with a respectful curtsey;" then "quietly, and without being told, unloosed her pinafore, and the teacher instantly and sharply inflicted on her neck a dozen strokes with the bunch of twigs." The teacher calls her "guilty of slatternly habits," though as Burns herself later admits this refers to the fact that she is careless, forgets the rules, and reads books like Samuel Johnson's *Rasselas* when she should be studying her lessons. "I cannot *bear* to be subjected to systematic arrangements," she confesses. The ritual of punishment instituted by Brocklehurst is meant to humiliate Burns, to suppress her independence of mind and imagination. Burns cannot *bear* the "systematic" even as she's being hurt for her rebellion.

A punishment for all the girls is the miserable food. At her first breakfast, ravenous and faint, Jane hears the older girls whispering, "Disgusting! The porridge is burnt again!" Still she is so hungry that she devours a couple of spoonful's only to realize she was eating "a nauseous mess." Soon, "Breakfast was over, and none had breakfasted." Since this is a religious school, each meal ends with a prayer, or, as Jane with bitter irony puts it, "Thanks being returned for what we had not got." Brocklehurst's school is bent on starving its pupils. We're told that the cook, Mrs. Harden (her name an obvious pun), is "a woman after Mr. Brocklehurst's own heart."

Brontë was convinced she had been physically damaged by her time at Cowan Bridge. Gaskell points out that should any teacher have voiced complaints on the subject, Wilson would reply to the effect that "the children were to be trained up to regard higher things than dainty pampering of the appetite, and . . . he lectured them on the sin of caring over-much for carnal things." In Brontë's novel Brocklehurst echoes these sentiments. The cook at Cowan Bridge during Charlotte's time there was dirty and careless, serving sour milk, the "meat . . . a greasy stew with alien bodies floating in it." To the students the whole place seemed to be pervaded by "the odor of rancid fat." On Saturdays she served a kind of pie made from all the uneaten scraps of food from the "dirty and disorderly larder" accumulated during the week.

All is done in the name of religion. The ironic boast on the stone tablet over the door to Lowood cites Matthew's Gospel: "Let your light shine before men that they may see your good works, and glorify your Father which is in heaven." Brontë knew her Bible. She knew that almost all of Jesus' teaching recommends private, even secret charity, while he frequently excoriates public boasting about one's virtue. But Brocklehurst has found a text to justify his pride. He commends himself on the show of his charity, despite its utter baselessness. This is religion, Brocklehurst style: "Sundays were dreary days," Jane recalls, as she recounts marching miles from Brocklehurst's church and a wind that "almost flayed the skin from our faces." The late afternoon would be crowned by the "famished great girls" who would "menace the little ones out of their portion" of the scanty evening meal. During her stay at Cowan Bridge, Charlotte was "the youngest and the smallest girl in the school" and victim to the treatment Jane narrates: "Many a time I have shared between two claimants the precious morsel of brown bread distributed at tea-time; and after relinquishing to a third, half the contents of my mug of coffee, I have swallowed the remainder with an accompaniment of secret tears, forced from me by the exigency of hunger." The practices of this Christian school have taught the larger and stronger to turn on the smaller and weaker and to take from them even the little which they have.

Brontë depicts the inner spring for many of Wilson's "disagreeable qualities, his spiritual pride, his love of power, his ignorance of human nature and consequent want of tenderness" in a celebrated scene when his stand-in character, Brocklehurst, visits the school. As Gaskell puts it, Wilson's "love of authority seems to have led to a great deal of unnecessary and irritating *meddling*," and on this day Brocklehurst catches sight of poor Julia Severn's curly red hair and commands it to "be cut off entirely." Then, turning on the other girls, he announces, "All those top-knots must be cut off." To the quiet protest of the head teacher Miss Temple, "Julia's hair curls naturally . . . " he responds, "[W]e are not to conform to nature . . . my mission is to mortify in these girls the lusts of the flesh." Brontë makes it clear that this form of religion is unnatural; it strives to kill what is natural and pleasing and needed. Here we get to the heart of one of the novel's central arguments, and an argument that enraged many mid-Victorian readers. The wry but considered comment by the famous poet Elizabeth Barrett Browning aptly encapsulates what many thought that *Jane Eyre* expresses: a vision "half savage & half freethinking." Indeed, to be natural is perhaps to be quasi-savage and certainly half freethinking.

To show how close the girls are to sinfulness, Brocklehurst turns on Jane. Recalling Mrs. Reed's accusation, he decides to make an example of her. He asks the girls to look carefully at her. "Who would think that the Evil One has already found a servant and agent in her?" His invective mirrors Wilson's *The Child's Friend* (1828) as it sternly warns the erring: "Are you living neglectful of God, forgetful of prayer, and ripening in sin? . . . What, oh what will become of you, should death strike an unexpected blow?

> 'Tis dang'rous to provoke a God,
> Whose power and vengeance none can tell;
> One stroke of his almighty rod
> Can send young sinners quick to hell."

Similarly, Brocklehurst goes on to warn the students that Jane is "an interloper and an alien." They must be on their guard around her and shun her because "this girl is—a liar!" Here the rebellious novelist, the pale and slender daughter of a clergyman, defiantly depicts a hypocritical priest, terrified of women's bodies to the point of seeking to mutilate them—"all . . . must be cut off." She now has him falsely accuse a child before the whole institution endeavoring to alienate them from her, using the language and imagery of scripture to accuse her of exactly that fault which Jane has previously denied. Is it all a bit "savage" and "half freethinking"? Certainly. It's a difficult fight they're engaged in. Forced to stand in front of everyone "on a pedestal of infamy," Jane struggles to master "the rising hysteria" moving through her, and lifting up her head "took a firm stand on the stool." Striking a courageous pose, the little girl confronts everyone and steels herself for the worst.

When the span of time for her to endure this exposure has ended, when Jane, now left alone, abandons herself to tears wishing to die, her friend Helen comes to her through "the long, vacant room." She brings "coffee and bread," sacramental succor for Jane's despair, and again as with Bessie in sisterhood she consoles her. As always in this novel, Charlotte is remembering her sisters, Emily and Anne, and their shared life together.

Brontë remembers another sister as well. During the afternoon of her first full day at Lowood, Jane Eyre finds herself sent to the school garden—it's the end of January, "all was wintry blight and brown decay . . ." While the strong girls run about and play games, "sundry pale and thin ones herded together for shelter and warmth in the veranda," where frequently she hears "the sound of a hollow cough." Any mid-Victorian reader would sense in the details of this scene the implicit warnings of incipient illness and death.

It is here Jane first meets Helen Burns in the cold afternoon air apart from the others reading *Rasselas*. As Jane recalls, "her occupation touched a chord of sympathy somewhere." Jane senses a kinship with Helen. Both, she can already see, are quiet, thoughtful, and involved in books. But Charlotte wishes to imply more. As early as 1830, in one of her first youthful writings, Brontë provides these words to her narrator: "It is the fashion nowadays to put no faith whatsoever in supernatural appearances or warnings. I am, however, a happy exception to the general rule. And firmly believe in everything of the kind." Like him, Jane has been fearful of the ghostly return of those who though dead are troubled by continued injustice to the living. In this scene Brontë introduces her heroine to the figure of her dead sister Maria.

When Charlotte was an adolescent and student at Roe Head in

the early 1830s, she would talk with Ellen Nussey about her two dead sisters, Maria and Elizabeth. Her love for them was intense; a kind of adoration. "She described Maria as a little mother among the rest, superhuman in goodness and cleverness." But what touched her most of all "were the revelations of her suffering." Charlotte recalled "her prematurely-developed and remarkable intellect, as well as the mildness, wisdom, and fortitude of her character." Maria was a great reader of newspapers from a very young age, and visitors marveled at her ability to discuss current affairs at great length in a lively and engaged fashion.

Elizabeth Gaskell's account pictures Maria as "grave, thoughtful, and quiet, to a degree beyond her years," shadowed by her oncoming death. Unable to enjoy the simple pleasures of childhood, she was already living "the deeper life of reflection." This gloomy portrait fits Helen Burns who is, trait for trait, virtue for virtue, Brontë's portrait of her older sister. As she wrote to her publisher: "she was real enough: I have exaggerated nothing here: I abstained from recording much that I remember respecting her, lest the narrative should sound incredible." Charlotte created Helen in part to record the truth about Maria's life and suffering. Gaskell writes with great sympathy about this. "Helen Burns is as exact a transcript of Maria Brontë as Charlotte's wonderful power of reproducing character could give her. Her heart, to the latest day on which we met, still beat with unavailing indignation at the worrying and the cruelty to which her gentle, patient, dying sister had been subjected."

It is in Brontë's account of the "cruelty" Maria suffered at Cowan Bridge that we encounter both Charlotte's intense love for her sister and the curbs and limits which she imposed upon her novel. Yes, we have the scene in which Miss Scatcherd—the woman's name was actually Miss Andrews—strikes Helen with a bundle of sticks. However, there was much that Brontë chose not to include. The most remarkable example of this intentional omission was recalled years later by a school friend. One morning Maria, suffering from illness, had a blister (i.e., acidic ointment spread on the skin to draw out diseased fluids) applied to one side and when the wake-up bell was rung, she moaned out that she was so ill, she wanted to stay in bed. However Miss Andrews was nearby so "the sick child began to dress, shivering with cold, as . . . she slowly put on her black worsted stocking over her thin white legs." Abruptly Andrews bolted from her room, grabbed "the sick and frightened girl . . . by the arm, on the side to which the blister had been applied, and by one vigorous movement whirled her out into the middle of the floor, abusing her all the time for dirty and untidy habits. There she left her." Staggering to her feet, Maria managed to get dressed and then trembling and haltingly, she got down stairs to the school room, only to be punished for being late.

The tragedy of Maria's life haunted Charlotte. Her knowledge of what Maria had suffered, and that she had not been with her when Maria died, must have seemed a kind of betrayal, a fault which called out for expiation. The ghost of this past, like the ghost of Mr. Reed, haunted the dark red-room of Charlotte's inner consciousness. Sometimes this recurrent obsession took unexpected turns. One of Charlotte's best friends from Roe Head, Mary Taylor, recalled that early one morning Charlotte told her that she had been troubled the night before by a dream:

[S]he had been told that she was wanted in the drawing-room, and it was Maria and Elizabeth . . . she wished she had not dreamed, for it did not go on nicely; they were changed; they had forgotten what they used to care for. They were very fashionably dressed, and began criticizing the room, etc.

Brontë was fascinated by dreams and includes in the novel her own dramatic fictions of dreaming, such as Jane Eyre's premonitory dreams from Chapter XXI of a troubling infant, a presentiment of changes which are to occur in her life. However, this disturbing account is quite different in its laconic presentation. It has all the characteristics of an actual dream in the way it takes the dead sisters and makes them remote, censorious, and uncaring, emblematic perhaps of Charlotte's fears about the inadequacy of her past relationships to them and her guilt because she is still alive.

Charlotte went on, a few years later, in her fantasy Angria writings to invent characters and scenes which restage elements of her relationship to Maria, which are, if anything, even more unnerving than her dreams. In 1836 she wrote of a fictional character Jane Moore, quite different from Jane Eyre in almost every way. In one scene, however, on a moonlit evening she is alone in her father's grand house and, as in an abstracted reverie, she thinks about the death of her older sister years before. Jane Moore remembers "the rigid and lengthened corpse laid in its coffin on the hall-table . . . of the kiss that she herself was bidden to give the corpse, of the feeling which then first gushed into her childish and volatile heart that Harriet had left them for ever." Brontë had been reimagining the deaths of her sisters for years. The creation of Helen Burns gave her another opportunity to reincarnate Maria.

As Helen comforts Jane after Brocklehurst's cruel indictment of her as a liar, suddenly "another person came in. Some heavy clouds, swept from the sky by a rising wind, had left the moon bare: and her light, streaming in through a window near, shone full both on us and on the approaching figure which we at once recognized as Miss Temple."

It's a crucial moment in the novel and in Charlotte's inner life.

Maria Temple greeted Jane upon her arrival and has interceded again and again on behalf of the girls about their hunger. When Brocklehurst denigrates them, she has been a calm and caring presence in the background. On this night she seeks Jane and brings both girls to her apartment. She consoles Jane for her public shaming, calling her "my child" and putting her arm around her. She allows Jane to clear herself of being condemned as a liar by telling her life story and then she kisses her. She gives Jane and Helen tea and generous slices of cake so welcome to "our famished appetites"— thus countermanding the starvation of Lowood school's discipline through pleasure. At the end of the evening, she embraces them both in parting as "my children."

Miss Temple is another character reborn from Charlotte's past life. There were, in the Brontë family, two Marias. Her sister was named Maria after her mother who died when she was seven and Charlotte five. The novel has called forth this second restless spirit from the past. Illuminated by the moon, like the Greek goddess Diana, she comes to protect her virginal daughters, to feed, comfort, and counsel them.

Her mother haunted Charlotte as well. How could she not, dying slowly and painfully when Charlotte was living at home and was an intensely impressionable young child?

In the family she was remembered as lively, loving, and beautiful. Patrick kept and treasured Maria's love letters, written to him when they were courting, in which she wrote of her anticipation of the "sacred pleasure . . . [and] perfect and uninterrupted bliss" of their forthcoming marriage. In 1830 the fourteen-year-old Charlotte carefully copied an old profile portrait of her mother, subtly altering some of the details to picture her as a pert, youthful figure, her flattering curling hair naturally springing from a cap, her dress with a frilled collar exposing a long white neck and empire dress with a generous breast. Charlotte imbues Miss Temple with the warmth of her mother and has Temple represent everything Brocklehurst sought to repress and cut off.

In this scene of Jane with Helen and Miss Temple, Charlotte imagines what it might have been like if her mother and sisters had not died: time spent confiding in them, conversing over the sweetness of cake, and hearing her older sister and mother discuss their ideas and the books they had read. It is a moment to embrace them in fiction.

At Lowood, however, it is just a passing moment. As the weather warms and Jane's health improves, typhus invades the school. Lowood's physical environment is asserted as the cause of the illness; the fetid and poisoned air itself seems to carry sickness. The disease spreads quickly to many of the girls.

The cowardly Brocklehurst refuses to come near the school and the cook flees, replaced by a kinder one. Miss Temple courageously nurses the sick and dying girls. The recollections of a nurse who actually worked at Cowan Bridge describe a similar scene. She found the "girls lying about; some resting their aching heads on the table, others on the ground; all heavy-eyed, flushed, indifferent, and weary, with pains in every limb." Hovering over all, as she recalled, was a "peculiar odor," which indicated to her this was "the fever."

Helen, too, is ill, but not with typhus. Her constant cough tells us that hers is a different illness. Tuberculosis was already in the Brontë family. Sister Maria was dangerously ill from it in February of 1825; taken home she died of it on May 6, age eleven. Elizabeth too was ill with it and returned May 31. It is not clear whether Charlotte and Emily returned to observe Elizabeth dying; her death came June 15, age ten. Charlotte had just turned nine years old.

At eleven at night Jane finds her way to Helen in Miss Temple's room guided by what has already become the highly symbolic "light of the unclouded summer moon." Driven by feelings of sisterhood, she is overwhelmed by her impulse: "I must embrace her before she died, – I must give her one last kiss, – exchange with her one last word." Brontë is now able through imagination—notice the repeated need of "I must"—to atone for her former absence and be with her sister Maria for her last hours of life, looked over and comforted by the lingering presence of her remembered mother. It is Maria as Helen who calls her to "nestle" together and puts her arm around her. It is Maria as Helen who consoles Charlotte: "the illness which is removing me is not painful; it is gentle and gradual; my mind is at rest." She voices a belief in a loving God as a "mighty, universal Parent" and in a "region of happiness" after death.

Helen's last words are of concern about Jane: "Are you warm, darling?" After a kiss, they fall asleep embracing.

The next morning Miss Temple returns from the sick room to find Jane, "my face against Helen Burns' shoulder, my arms around her neck. I was asleep, and Helen was—dead."

The powerful confluence of private, indeed secret, emotions in this scene—guilt and grief because of the past and her former incapacity and inaction are now replaced by an imaginative transformation of the "truth" into a deeper "Truth" of sisterhood, love, and consolation. These are precisely the kinds of profound parallels to her life that Charlotte Brontë refused to acknowledge in public. Yet she could not help but embed the innermost feelings of her heart into her fiction. At points such as this, Brontë's need to write a secret history is most evident in the contradictory character of her impulses. She needs to write publicly about her loss, sorrow, and desire—these emotions give the scene its power—and yet she doesn't wish readers to know they are her emotions, emerging from the tragedies of her childhood. As an artist she achieves a dramatic balance between a truth that is historically based and, at the same time, a Truth that is from a compensatory imagination which atones for and consoles what had been a desolation.

If life had been unjust to her in the tragedies of her childhood, Brontë now corrects that injustice through the recuperative power of her imagination.

4

The First Girl

Time moves quickly after the death of Helen Burns. Jane Eyre claims this will not be a "regular autobiography" and skips over the next eight years of what Jane calls her "insignificant" life. In passing, she notes that the deaths of several Lowood students prompt public indignation, and the school is so completely reformed that she remains for six years as a pupil and for two as a teacher.

Charlotte Brontë's own life was far different. While it is true that Cowan Bridge School was reformed, it wasn't until 1832 that it was moved to a new and more salubrious site, long after Patrick Brontë brought Charlotte and Emily back to Haworth.

From August of 1825 to January 1831, Charlotte spent not in a boarding school, but living with her family. When she was almost fifteen, she returned to formal education in a private girls school run by Miss Wooler: Roe Head. While she remained there for a scant year and a half, leaving in June of 1832 to live at home again, her world had changed. She had made new friends at Roe Head. Young women from families of substantial wealth and education, possessing good minds, high spirits, and expectations for the future. They corresponded, sent each other presents, visited each other's homes, and went on short trips together. Altogether between the ages of fifteen and nineteen Charlotte matured into the grown woman we see replicated in her heroine Jane Eyre.

Charlotte's and Jane's personal development are interesting to compare. As we scan the important aspects of this crucial process, we can see some striking instances of the novelist selecting from remembered experiences, sometimes reporting the facts of her past, and at other times letting her imagination freely project choices and consequences that had not been a part of her life.

⹂

This process of development is anticipated quite early in the novel. Following her confrontation with Mrs. Reed, Jane escapes into the wintry garden at Gateshead whispering to herself, "What shall I do?" The servant Bessie finds her and wonders at this "little, roving, solitary thing." As they talk, Bessie notes the frank, self-confident, and dispassionate tone of Jane's remarks and says, "You little sharp thing! you've got a new way of talking. What makes you so venturesome and hardy?" The child's victory over the older, dominating Mrs. Reed has brought forth a sureness in judgment and a kind of intrepid fearlessness. The way Jane talks suggests to Bessie that this child has a new toughness and a willingness to take risks.

The novel's readers already know this voice. The Jane Eyre who tells her life story is in her early thirties. While she can evoke the emotions of a moment from many years earlier as she writes, she can also look back with the wisdom of experience and of a mind and spirit that time and challenges have shaped. Taunted, hit, and injured by John Reed, the well-read little ten-year-old can cry out, "You are like a murderer—you are like a slave-driver—you are like the Roman emperors!" At the same time the narrator can wryly remark of that moment of fury and indignation that she had read Goldsmith's *History of Rome* and had "formed my opinion of Nero, Caligula, &c." Young Jane, struggling to make sense of the injustice in her life, makes what now seems to her more mature self a slightly amusing and exaggerated parallel, and Jane Eyre, as narrator, can judge with wit both her youthful self and the boorish opponent she confronts on that dark, formative afternoon of the first chapter. Her "way of talking" frames and shapes her account of her life, constantly suggesting to the reader that though seemingly small, roving, and solitary, she will, in the face of seemingly insuperable obstacles, achieve what she chooses.

For Charlotte, life at Haworth, after Cowan Bridge, became a place that nurtured the free development of her mind and voice through reading and lively discussion while at the same time offering her the opportunity to playfully liberate her imagination to express itself through drawing and writing. We can see this happening, as well as how the voice of Jane Eyre begins to emerge, by looking at a couple of Brontë's writings from 1829 when Charlotte was twelve and thirteen years old.

In an utterly charming prose snapshot, her second earliest surviving manuscript dated March 12, 1829, written a month before her thirteenth birthday, which she titled "THE HISTORY OF THE YEAR 1829," Charlotte begins describing a typical afternoon at home. Papa and Branwell have gone to the nearby town of Keighley to pick up the latest copy of the *Leeds Intelligencer*. It's one of three newspapers, she notes proudly, that they take each week, while also borrowing from a neighbor his copy of *Blackwood's Magazine*, which she calls "the most able periodical there is." The servant Tabby is washing up in the kitchen. Anne is looking at the cakes Tabby has just baked. Emily is in the next room brushing the carpet, while Charlotte writes at the kitchen table. *Blackwood's* makes her think of the Brontë children's imitations of that magazine in their fantasy writings. She lists and dates them, calling them plays, and remarking, "All our plays are very strange ones."

It's important to note, first, that Patrick Brontë, father of this remarkable family, was a very public man. Much more than simply a parish priest in Haworth, Patrick frequently argued his views on the most hotly debated issues of the moment in local papers. Between January 15 and February 5 of 1829 he had published three letters in the *Leeds Intelligencer* controversially arguing for the Catholic Emancipation bill as "an antidote" to the political extremism currently stirring in Ireland, which, he feared, could lead to "popular violence" and the danger of Irish secession from Great Britain. Juliet Barker's astute analysis of his position points out that while what he wrote was contrary to the convictions of most of his local political allies, he had taken a position in favor of limited rights for Irish Catholics, whom he himself did not trust, for the sake of preserving the unity of the Kingdom. The figure which their father thus struck was of intense interest to his children. This issue, like many, was vigorously discussed at home. Patrick wishes to pick up the paper on this day at least in part to see what the most recent news reporting has to say about it. The king's speech in favor of Catholic emancipation in February had been followed by Robert Peel, at the time home secretary, introducing "The Roman Catholic Relief Act" in the House of Commons, and by March it was before the House of

Lords. It was the burning issue of the day, and something Patrick was deeply invested in.

Charlotte frames Patrick's intellectual and political activity within the sweetly mundane activities of home life. Her references to the children's fantasy plays and their strangeness then leads to Charlotte recording a crucial moment three years earlier. In June of 1826 Patrick had brought from Leeds a birthday present for Branwell, a box of toy soldiers. The next morning his siblings began snatching them up as their own and naming them. Charlotte assures the reader hers is "the prettiest of the whole, and the tallest, and the most perfect in every part." She names him the Duke of Wellington. Branwell, always the ready antagonist, names his "Buonaparte." Thus into their childish play the young Brontës weave their own rivalries—whose is the best?—and protagonists from recent history which was so much a part of their intellectual world. In her writing, Charlotte illustrates her early delight in the particulars of daily life—those tempting cakes now cooling on the kitchen table—in the picturing of individual people—the young Anne sniffing at them—and a precocious self-confidence in judgment that shows her eagerly open to intellectual risk: *Blackwells* is the best, no question.

In the voluminous writings that soon follow there is frequently a sense of fun, yet coupled with a remarkable range of allusions, not only to contemporary politics but also to Scipio Africanus, Socrates, Ovid, Virgil, and Herodotus. The Brontë children ransacked their father's library sharing what they learned with each other.

A story titled "An Adventure in Ireland," written just over a month later and dated April 28, 1829, already illustrates Charlotte's self-confident narrative voice, while uncannily anticipating several of the crucial elements of *Jane Eyre*. With the privilege of hindsight we can see the adult novelist in training. The unnamed first-person narrator visiting a remote part of Ireland is impressed by the beauty of the evening and a lake "in which the reflection of the pale moon was not disturbed by the smallest wave." Over the nearby village "the grey robe of twilight" is stealing. Nothing breaks the stillness of the scene but "the hum of the distant village" and the "sweet song of the nightingale in the wood." Brontë shows that she is already capable of evoking the quality of time, place, and the mood of a specific moment. She unconsciously anticipates the moment in chill twilight when Jane and Mr. Rochester first meet.

The scene set, the narrator is greeted by a polite local who invites him to spend the night in his "castle," which turns out to be in some ways quite like the future Thornfield, a large building superintended by an old lady, anticipating Mrs. Fairfax, sitting by the fireside knitting, her tortoise-shell cat nearby. Retiring for the night, the narrator is accosted by a boy who warns the room is haunted, much like the red-room at Gateshead, by the "ould masther's ghost," and as the narrator falls asleep, he thinks he can see "something white through the darkness," just as Jane Eyre will later.

His ensuing nightmares begin with a skeleton in a white sheet which leads him, paralyzed into silence by fear, to scenes such as an enormous waterfall in "clouds of spray" rolling down "tremendous precipices" and then into mines deep under the ocean where, despite the magnificence of the subterranean corridors, he feels fear and terror because the sea is raging overhead, threatening to overwhelm everything. The sequence ends with a desert cave in which a "royal lion" wakes, fixes him with its terrible eyes, and delivers a "tremendous roar of fierce delight." Just as with Charlotte's later narratives of her dream reveries at Roe Head, here too the laconic Irish boy suddenly wakes the sleeper where the morning sun now illuminates "the little old-fashioned room at the top of O'Callaghan Castle."

There is a lot of fun here, the thrills and chills of the gothic tradition, along with tales of exploration in distant lands. But almost certainly running beneath the surface is a string of dream-visions of the dangers in Catholic emancipation. We are in Ireland, Patrick Brontë's birth place, and we find it is haunted by a seemingly dead past that returns as a spectral presence. Charlotte uses the terrifying ocean, which seems to be about to overwhelm the glittering arches of the palatial mines, as an allegory for the threats of national rebellion, only to be replaced by what must be the British monarchical lion fiercely delighting in the assertion of his primacy.

The Jane Eyre who will tell the stories of the red-room, of the mysteriously locked third-floor room at Thornfield, who will describe premonitory thunderstorms that snap trees in half and the terrifying desolation of a solitary wanderer in the moors is taking shape as Charlotte Brontë begins to find elements of her distinctive voice.

Jane remains at Lowood. From her first days there she had hoped to make friends, to "earn respect, and win affection." After Helen's death, Jane pursues her studies with "a desire to excel in all," seeking to please her teachers as she availed herself of "the advantages offered me." With time, she rises to become "the first girl of the first class."

After Charlotte's six happy years at home, Patrick Brontë decided to enroll her in the Roe Head school. For Charlotte this second displacement from home and family was difficult and challenging—not as abrupt and overwhelming as being sent as an eight-year-old to Cowan Bridge, but nevertheless not very easy. There she was to face some of the challenges she later presents to her fictional self, Jane Eyre, but also difficulties that Jane never had to confront.

On the day of Charlotte's arrival, January 17, 1831, bitterly homesick already, she was discovered by another, similarly unhappy new girl, who later remembered her in their first encounter as "a silent, weeping, dark little figure in the large bay-window." She seemed, to Ellen Nussey, "anything but *pretty*." Her hair was "dry and frizzy-looking, screwed up in tight little curls, showing features that were all the plainer from her exceeding thinness and want of complexion." Mary Taylor, who met her too on this first day, recalled Charlotte's arrival with equal vividness. "I first saw her coming out of a covered cart, in very old-fashioned clothes and looking very cold and miserable." In the classroom she looked like a "little, old woman, so short-sighted that she always appeared to be seeking something, and moving her head from side to side to catch a sight of it. She was very shy and nervous and spoke with a strong Irish accent."

School for the adolescent Charlotte was, just as it was later to be for the fictive Jane Eyre, an opportunity—a means to prove and transform herself. At the same time it was a burden. Charlotte was, as Ellen Nussey put it, "an object of expense to those at home" and so had to use every moment of study to "fit herself for governess life." This anxiety bore down hard on the fifteen year old. She couldn't play or amuse herself like the other girls. In the evenings when they gathered around the fire she would kneel close to the window busy with her studies, and this would last so long that the other girls teased her about "seeing in the dark." The scene in *Jane Eyre*'s first paragraphs with Jane seated at the window on a cold, rainy afternoon is thus partly a recollection of Charlotte's early months as an unproven student, to some degree marginalized by the oddity of her appearance, her short-sightedness, her almost foreign accent.

Jane Eyre and Charlotte both felt the difficulty of being different. Through success in their studies, both were to earn respect and friendship from their fellow students and their teachers. Mary Taylor was struck by Charlotte's wide-ranging knowledge. She was already familiar with the passages of poetry students had to memorize and could explain to the others who the authors were, the texts they came from, and would "sometimes repeat a page or two, and tell us the plot." Mary gratefully recalled, "She made poetry and drawing . . . exceedingly interesting to me."

Within months Charlotte was recognized as a top student in the school. Like Jane she became "first girl." Both succeeded through diligent hard work and self-control—though to a more critical eye their rewards are meager: a few school awards and trophies, things that soon melt into insignificance when confronted with life's real-world challenges. From the start Ellen sees Charlotte as being trained for an unrewarding job: being a governess, the same role Jane Eyre was later to take up.

That Charlotte was already a prolific writer of poetry and prose narratives remained a closely guarded secret from even her closest school friends, but her parallel dedication to drawing was well known to them. It was one of the skills Roe Head students were taught. She did detailed depictions of flowers and plants, copies of portraits of people's faces, and some very successful landscapes, even a charming depiction of the school building. In this way friends recognized early on that Brontë aspired not to be a governess, but rather an artist. When she was unhappy with a picture, she would destroy it, then "cheerfully set to work again intent on achieving her ideal if possible." Had Brontë permitted Ellen to see her secret writings, her close friend would have understood even more fully Charlotte's artistic ambition.

Jane Eyre, too, from her youthful days at Lowood school was an eager and intent visual artist. She tells us how her skill at drawing equals her success in the classroom and lists "the spectacle of ideal drawings" that she plans to execute, "freely penciled houses and trees, picturesque rocks and ruins, . . . sweet paintings of butterflies hovering over unblown roses, of birds picking at ripe cherries, of wrens' nests enclosing pearl-like eggs, wreathed about with young ivy sprays." Pictures very like Charlotte's Roe Head drawings in subject and planned execution. And perhaps listed here ironically since these subjects are of a particularly cloying character, the sort required of proper women students and without a trace of innovation or challenge. In Chapter Seven we will take a close look at Jane Eyre's later drawings, which Brontë describes in detail—pictures completely different from these stereotyped early works, radically new in conception and execution.

When Jane leaves Lowood she leaves behind whatever friends she may have made. She presents herself to the reader as almost completely alone. The only person who remembers and takes any interest at all in her is Bessie, the servant from Gateshead. Things were very different for Charlotte Brontë. Back at Haworth, she returned to the excitement of writing shared with Branwell, as they continued their chronicles of the fantasy world Angria, and expanded the range of her own world and experience. Shortly after leaving Miss Wooler's school in June of 1832, the sixteen-year-old Charlotte visited the homes of her two best school friends. The Nusseys lived in Rydings, at Birstall, an old house with a castellated roof line and extensive gardens. When Branwell accompanied Charlotte on her second visit, as Ellen later recalled, "he was in wild ecstasy" with everything. He loved the turret-roofed house, the fine chestnut trees on the lawn (one of which was iron "girthed," having been split by storms but still flourishing in great majesty), and a large rookery that gave a good background to the house. He told Charlotte "he was leaving her in Paradise." The split chestnut tree was to make a dramatic reappearance in Chapter XXIII of *Jane Eyre*.

Ellen's was an extensive and lively family, and Charlotte, accustomed to the intimacy and familiarity of Haworth, was painfully shy among them. Still, she got to know them all, and in the years to come she would discuss each of them and their lives in her letters to Ellen—Henry, for instance, who became a clergyman (we shall hear more of him later), and George, whose encroaching mental illness led to his becoming permanently kept in an asylum. He certainly was on Charlotte's mind as she began to imagine the fate of Bertha Mason Rochester. At the time, the Nusseys were still financially prosperous, and Ellen's future promised to be far more attractive than Brontë's.

She later visited her friend Mary Taylor at her home, the Red House, a large, Georgian brick building in Gomersal surrounded by lawns and a grove of walnut trees. There Charlotte, a lifelong conservative, ardent admirer of the Duke of Wellington and his opposition to the Reform Act of 1832, entered into lively discussions with the Taylors, convinced political radicals, about the burning issues of the day. A third visit took her to the home of her father's friends, the Atkinsons, whose vicarage was called Green House. Her anxiety among strangers returning, she retreated to the garden whenever she could. Charlotte's intermittent shyness during these visits anticipated Jane Eyre's marginal position at Rochester's house parties.

Four years later, in June of 1836, she visited another Roe Head alumna, Amelia Walker, whose family home Lascelles Hall, at least part of which was from the sixteenth century, included large, "'park-like' grounds." In a subsequent letter Charlotte attacked Amelia as "monstrously gracious" during her visit, "changing her character every half hour." Amelia had become exemplary of how money and status lead to insincere role playing and mindless vanity, pretending at one moment to be "the sweet sentimentalist," then a moment later "the reckless rattler." Sometimes the question was 'Shall I look prettiest lofty?' and again 'Would not tender familiarity suit me better?' At one moment she affected to inquire after her old school-acquaintance the next she was detailing anecdotes of High Life." Charlotte found her brother an "incorrigible <u>Booby</u>."

In these years Charlotte Brontë had firsthand experience of the adult world she would depict in *Jane Eyre*. She saw, visited, and explored a mélange of country houses whose architecture and interior decorations provided hints for her future invention, Thornfield, as well as the gardens, out buildings, and landscapes where Jane Eyre is to meet Mr. Rochester for their ever-more intimate and revelatory conversations. Charlotte Brontë was strolling the grounds, seeing the arriving guests, being the uncomfortable visitor, and formed her judgments accordingly. Echoing Jane Eyre's satirical description of the house party at Thornfield, Charlotte, writing to Ellen Nussey in January 1847, summarizes her experiences: "As to society I don't understand much about it – . . . it seems to me a very strange, complicated affair indeed – wherein Nature is turned upside down – . . . eternal and tedious botheration is their notion of happiness – sensible pursuits their ennui."

The tart frankness of these letters is absolutely typical of the written voice both of Brontë and of her narrator Jane Eyre. It's how she presented herself to her two best friends in their frequent and lively correspondence. Let us look for a moment at a couple of examples taken from letters of 1834, two years after Charlotte has left Roe Head.

In a letter of February 20, 1834, Charlotte writes to Ellen that she has recently received a letter from Mary telling of Ellen's departure for an extended visit to London. Charlotte teases Ellen for what appears to her to be an excessively calm reaction to a city that "has drawn exclamations of astonishment" from world travelers in order not to appear "country bred," and she wonders if Ellen has seen any of the "Great Personages" then in London for the sitting of Parliament—including Charlotte's hero the Duke of Wellington. Living a relatively isolated life in Haworth, and eagerly curious to visit the metropolis she has read so much about, Brontë suggests how differently she would approach such an opportunity.

And yet in her next surviving letter from June 19, she celebrates the fact that Ellen returns home as natural and unsophisticated as when she first left. She assesses what this implies: "I see no affectation in your letters, no trifling no frivolous contempt of plain, and weak admiration of showy persons and things." Note the intimacy, and the confident certitude in judgment of Brontë's voice here, so much like Jane Eyre's. Charlotte claims a skill in exploring the "turning, windings inconsistencies and obscurities" of human nature. Unbeknownst to her friend, Charlotte's by now voluminous fiction writing suggests that her boast has substance. The future author of *Jane Eyre* and *Villette* is staking her claim to special insights into the human heart.

In a third letter, from July 4, Brontë writes regretfully of the news that the Nussey family may have to sell their home. "Rydings," she observes, unconsciously anticipating her own imagined Thornfield that is to come, "is a pleasant spot, one of the old family Halls of England, surrounded by Lawn and wood-land, speaking of past times and suggesting (to me at least) happy feelings." Jane Eyre will share a similar rueful retrospective when she finds herself torn from Thornfield and Mr. Rochester by her own willed decision.

1825 to 1835 were thus happy years of growth and personal development for Brontë, a period in which her schoolmates and friends came to know her as remarkably knowledgeable, witty, frankly affectionate, and self-confident. A woman becoming, indeed, in some respects more and more like the Jane Eyre who sums up briefly her similar development at the fictional Lowood. For both, however, this period of gestation had to end. At age eighteen Jane finds herself yearning for "liberty" and prepared to accept a new form of "servitude" by taking the job of governess. Similarly, the economic needs of her family lead Charlotte, age nineteen, to take her first paying job. This event opens up a much more complex and frequently very unhappy phase in her life. Crucial to Charlotte will be the continuing love and support of her family, particularly her sisters Emily and Anne, as well as the sympathetic and supportive respect and affection of her old school friends. Jane Eyre will have to take this next step on her own.

5

A Situation

The reproach of her "dependence" had been a "painful and crushing" sing-song in Jane Eyre's earliest memories. Orphaned at an early age, without any family or any money, though she is technically middle class, she can only hope for a "humble" place and to make herself quietly "agreeable."

In seeking a new form of "servitude," this is what Jane wants: a situation. That is what she is offered by Mrs. Fairfax, who replies to an advertisement Jane has placed in a local newspaper. Jane is assured there is "but one pupil, a little girl under ten years of age . . ." and she imagines this Mrs. Fairfax "in a black gown and widow's cap," hopefully "a model of elderly English respectability." However, the term "situation" can mean quite different things. A job, yes, but also an alternative Jane actually considers: "some scrape!" Both await her at Thornfield Hall.

Jane's impulsive wish to dramatically change her life directly mirrors one of Charlotte Brontë's attempts to break free of the constraints imprisoning her. During the Christmas holidays of 1836, back home from teaching at Roe Head, she wrote to poet laureate Robert Southey about her dreams of being a writer, including two examples of her recent poetry in a letter. Her turn to this literary father figure led to unhappy consequences. Southey replied a little more than two months later in terms cautiously amiable but shattering. "The day-dreams in which you habitually indulge," he wrote, "are likely to induce a distempered state of mind," and he warned her that pursuing her Angrian fantasies would in time make her incapable of doing anything further as a writer. For Charlotte Brontë, who found this imagined world to be her only escape from what was often a dreary daily life, his was a heart-stopping prohibition. The warning that this daydreaming might lead to a kind of madness—"a distempered . . . mind"—could only feed her anxiety about her current mental state.

Southey then concluded, in language he could never have imagined would make him more than a century later a perfect example of patriarchal opposition to feminist ambition, "Literature cannot be the business of a woman's life: & it ought not to be. The more she is engaged in her proper duties, the less leisure will she have for it, even as an accomplishment & a recreation." The conflict between the domestic and familial responsibilities Charlotte was expected to fulfill versus the creative ambition and ardent passions that stirred her could not have been stated more absolutely; the phrase "proper duties" severely voicing a sense of cultural and religiously sanctioned certitude.

In a poem written two months later, Brontë pictured a "restless eye" that looms over her solitude, and an inner life trying to conceal a "secret" which is constantly revealed by her smothered sighs and silent tears. While these lines may form a part of one of the love stories in her Angrian tales, they readily suggest as well her anxiety about Southey's chilling assertions that seem, as the poem goes on, to now wake her from some kind of "wild dream." Desperately, she hopes, "Pride should sometimes speak" and "that bondsman break / Its self-locked chain ere yet too late." Chained talent—notably, a "self-locked" chain suggesting how fully she has accepted and internalized Southey's certitude—leading to a haunted solitude of unfulfilled dreams, stall the poem's speaker, who in the last stanzas must turn to prayer and a hope that a divine "Father" will take her to a "haven" beyond this present life where grief can no longer "vex my home!" These theological consolations are a regular feature in the poetry of Charlotte's sister Emily and in their father's writing as well. But they were scant comfort for the unhappiness of Charlotte Brontë's daily life.

Charlotte, age nineteen, had returned to the Roe Head July 29, 1835, as a teacher, and had been working there for a year and a half when she wrote the letter to Southey. She would remain there until December of 1838. For much of this three-and-a-half-year span she was angrily unhappy. Scorning her pupils and prevented by long hours at work from continuing the narratives and poems she shared with her brother Branwell, Charlotte lived a life of nervous fatigue and desperation.

Jane Eyre presents her two years as a teacher in an idealized summary of personal development and adaptation, in sharp contrast to Charlotte's own experience. However, immediately beneath the surface of what Jane says one easily recognizes echoes of Charlotte's unhappy past experience. Jane comments that she "remained an inmate" at Lowood, where her "life was uniform: but not unhappy because it was not inactive." The term "inmate" captures not only Jane's but also Charlotte's sense that teaching and boarding in a rural school for girls was not very different from imprisonment. The uniformity of life suggests disciplinary rigor and sameness that leads to Jane's double negatives "not unhappy . . . not inactive" which unsuccessfully gloss over her frustration. Both young women seek to "avail" themselves of opportunities that they really don't seek. Jane's description of her teaching as "discharged with zeal" is a sugar-coated denial of Charlotte's detestation of her Roe Head pupils whom she characterized as "fat-headed oafs." There is no question that when she came to invent John, Eliza, and Georgiana Reed, Charlotte recalled her intense animus toward these children, and that it fueled Jane's angry, satirical attacks on them. While Jane claims to have achieved control over her earlier rages with "better-regulated feelings," Charlotte's writing from these years tells another story, of an emotional life in which "there was always excess." She was always "too excited or too despondent."

This revelatory comment comes from an essay Brontë wrote a few years after leaving Roe Head, and the essay, as a whole, captures the ultimate source of her dissatisfaction with teaching. In it, thinking about herself as a young pupil eager to recite long passages of poetry; diligently spending whole days executing drawings in fine detail, reveling in her years of spirited, collaborative writing, she had become convinced of "the difference which existed between me and most of the people who surrounded me . . . I believe that I have Genius." These remarks clearly voice her long-standing sense of herself. Struggling against the imposed presupposition from her earliest days that she was to be trained as a governess or teacher, Brontë, feeling deep within herself that she was destined for a very different life, could not help but feel that the demands of her current life were detestably wrong. The letter to Southey further illustrates how she felt. How could she assume, as she desperately writes in her "Roe Head Journal," "an air of kindness, patience & assiduity" in treating her students when she wonders "am I to spend all of the best part of my life in this wretched bondage, forcibly suppressing my rage at the idleness the apathy and the hyperbolical & most asinine stupidity" of the pupils? The burden was sometimes almost insupportable. One night, lying sleepless in bed, listening to students coming into the room "to get their curl-papers" and whispering about her, she felt as if "heavy weight laid across me . . . as if some huge animal had flung itself across me—a horrid apprehension quickened every pulse I had. I must get up I thought." But escape proved not so easy to achieve.

Hardest for Charlotte was the painful sense that she was being forced to abandon the creatures of her imagination because she was overwhelmed by the burden of her daily obligations. There is a whole cluster of poems from this period in which she laments the loss of the characters and fantasy lands she had once escaped to with her siblings. "But once again, but once again / I'll bid the strings awake . . ." from January of 1836 written during a holiday vacation from Roe Head is typical. She bids farewell, lamenting to her "comrades" that they must part. Of her favorite, Zamorna, she says:

> . . . he has held
> A lofty, burning lamp to me
> Whose rays surrounding darkness quelled
> And shewed me wonder, shadow free . . .

Indeed to her he had been a "god." Still he dwells "divine" in his "marble shrine," but now only a dream of past glory she rarely glimpses. Though she stopped writing fantasies set in Angria, Charlotte was not to lose sight of Zamorna. In Chapters Six and Seven we shall see how he returns to her, present in Mr. Rochester.

Charlotte gives Jane the same inner power—call it genius—that Charlotte claimed. One illustration of this is Jane's remarkable ability as a visual artist, and in Chapter Six we will scrutinize several of the pictures she has been creating during these Lowood years. But there is an even more convincing illustration of Jane's right to this claim in the very book we are reading. It is the "Autobiography" itself which constitutes the most powerful argument imaginable that Jane Eyre can insist that a "difference . . . existed between me and most of the people who surrounded me." The novel demonstrates her power as a writer on every page. In so doing it justifies Charlotte's desire to break free of Roe Head, and Jane's longing to follow the "white road" which she glimpses out of the window at Lowood, in search for the liberty she desires.

⁂

Paradoxically, Miss Wooler's invitation to Charlotte to return to the school where she had been such a promising student to join its faculty was almost certainly an act of kindness. She knew of the Brontës' straitened economic circumstances and giving a job to the oldest daughter was her way to help. Claire Harman in her recent biography of Charlotte writes with warm sympathy of Wooler, whose nephew described her as "'a keen-witted, ironical and very independent Yorkshire woman,' sensible, even-tempered and sensitive to the needs of her charges"—the type of woman who could readily serve Charlotte as a role model. In the evening Wooler typically chatted with her pupils telling stories, at times walking up and down the length of the Roe Head schoolroom "with the girls hanging about her 'delighted to listen to her, or have a chance of being nearest in the walk.'" As time passed, however, the supportive companionship of this kind woman could not allay what biographer Juliet Barker describes as Charlotte's "overwrought state of mind." The climax came during the Easter season of 1838 when, for sixteen days, Brontë was left on her own to run the school. A sign perhaps of Wooler's respect for Charlotte. But she was not up to the responsibility: "My health and spirits utterly failed me," she told Ellen Nussey, and a doctor urged her to return to Haworth "if I valued my life." She feels herself a "shattered wretch" who has somehow survived "weeks of mental and bodily anguish not to be described." The kindly apothecary Mr. Lloyd, who visits a similarly shattered Jane Eyre after the red-room experience, may come from this experience. More generally, Jane Eyre's extreme emotional states and particularly the crisis moments when she must break away from overwhelming inner oppression stem from Brontë's memories of these days when she had to flee.

⸎

Only eight months later Brontë finds herself in, if anything, worse circumstances. They would, again, provide her with powerful inspiration for her future novel.

Beginning life as a governess was far more unpleasant for Charlotte Brontë and her sister Anne than it was for Jane Eyre. When only a little more than eighteen years old, Anne served for nine months (April–December 1839) as governess for the Ingham family in charge of their two oldest children. Her novel, *Agnes Grey*, recounts her disillusionment as she begins to learn what being a governess actually entails.

It opens with its eponymous heroine ironically recalling her happy anticipations: "How delightful it would be to be a governess! To go out into the world; to enter upon a new life; to act for myself; to exercise my unused faculties; to try my unknown powers." In considering sources for John Reed, we have already met Agnes' pupil Tom Bloomfield who introduces himself by showing her his trapped birds that he happily tortures. His sister Mary Ann, a six-year-old child, ignores her teacher, literally lying on the floor much of the time. Their mother persistently sides with the children and limits Agnes' efforts to discipline them. A half year later, Anne Brontë became governess at Thorp Green Hall where she was happier and remained for several years. After she left she began writing her governess novel *Agnes Grey*, which Charlotte had read before starting *Jane Eyre*.

Years later Charlotte Brontë, discussing *Agnes Grey* with Elizabeth Gaskell, told her: "none but those who had been in the position of a governess could ever realize the dark side of 'respectable' human nature . . . daily giving way to selfishness and ill-temper, till its [i.e., "respectable human nature's"] conduct towards those dependent on it sometimes amount[s] to a tyranny." Here she echoes Jane Eyre's description of John Reed's "violent tyrannies," and she remembers as well the ruthless power of his mother Mrs. Reed. Charlotte thought about liberty and justice frequently throughout her adult life. In a letter from 1848, she repeats similar assertions saying that a governess lived "a life of inexpressible misery; tyrannized over, finding her efforts to please and teach utterly vain, chagrined, distressed, worried—so badgered so trodden-on, that she ceased almost at last to know herself . . . her oppressed mind . . . prisoned," and so became unable to imagine that other people might treat her with respect and affection. Here the whole repertoire of *Jane Eyre*'s first scenes— tyranny, shame, imprisonment—reappears in Charlotte's summary of what it means to be a governess. She remembered her experiences, and those of her sister Anne, as she sat down to write that novel's first chapters.

Charlotte's first "situation" as a temporary governess began in May 1839, at an estate named Stonegappe, a large house of three stories set on a hillside surrounded by woods, enjoying a vista in the distance of the valley of the River Aire. Charlotte was to care for a young girl and her brother—the stone-throwing son of the Sidgwick family we have seen as a model for John Reed. For the socially awkward and impoverished Brontë, at age twenty-three, the inferior position of governess in a wealthy family was an almost intolerable position, far worse than teaching at Roe Head. She was ignored by adult family members, charged with insolent and rebellious children, and denied respect by all, though she considered herself not only more than their equal in terms of intelligence and ability but also a potential writer of genius. She speaks vividly on the ambiguities of being a governess in a letter to her sister Emily, first acknowledging the attractions of living in the home of wealthy people: "The country, the house, and the grounds are . . . divine." However, for her none of this was available. Working as a governess took all her time. Viewing her as an employee drawing wages, the woman of the house, responsible to her husband to be an able manager of the staff and its expenses, Mrs. Sidgwick wasn't interested in befriending as an equal this poor clergyman's daughter or even in engaging her in conversation. Instead, like a good midcentury Victorian factory owner, she wanted to get as much work out of Charlotte, per hour, as she could. Of Mrs. Sidgwick Charlotte writes, "[she] . . . does not know my character & she does not wish to know it. I have never had five minutes of conversation with her since I came – except when she was scolding me . . . " What galls Brontë is not only Sidgwick's bossiness but also and, more importantly, her indifference to Charlotte as a person. And so when one of the Sidgwick children at dinner one day put his hand in Charlotte's saying, "I love 'ou, Miss Brontë," the mother broke in, before all the children in a tone of disdain, "Love the *governess*, my dear!"

Winifred Gérin, in her beautifully written biography of Brontë, pictures Charlotte in the Sidgwick's handsome country home during a "long summer evening when she sat alone, her lap filled with Mrs. Sidgwick's 'oceans of needlework' . . . no one from the noisy self-absorbed house-party below to share her solitude." Gérin goes on to tell us of Charlotte's private space, which she herself had explored.

> Charlotte's bedroom . . . had deep window seats and Georgian panes to its window-frames, and through them a lonely girl could look down unobserved on the arrivals and departures, the gentlemen on their horses and the ladies in their carriages, that animated the summer scene.

Judging herself to be the plausibly lively and witty equal of these people, Brontë could only feel the pain of her solitude. Her months at Stonegappe were, then, largely unhappy ones, despite her expensive accommodation and a "holiday" with the family in a residence near the opulent spa resort of Harrowgate. Charlotte left this employment in July.

What we now see is how much Brontë drew from these experiences as she began to write *Jane Eyre*, including the stone-throwing son, the feelings of alienation and solitude, and, most poignantly, the experience of a well-appointed, comfortable country home in which, like Jane Eyre later, Charlotte from the upper rooms watched people happily enjoying themselves utterly oblivious to her and to what she might have to offer.

Curiously and significantly, Brontë used her experiences of subor-
dination, exploitation, and humiliation not for Jane Eyre's work as a
governess, which she describes as easy and pleasant, but instead for
Jane's much earlier experiences at Gateshead Hall. The most dramatic
instance is the way she transforms Mrs. Sidgwick into Mrs. Reed.
This is Mrs. Reed: "A woman of robust frame, square-shouldered and
strong-limbed." She has a large face, "the under-jaw being much devel-
oped and very solid." Her brow is "low, her chin large and prominent."
She dresses well and has "a presence and port calculated to set off
handsome attire." Typically, Brontë, with her lifelong interest in issues
such as phrenology and the relationship of body to sensibility, finds
revelation in the close scrutiny of the physical details of this woman.
Her intractable will, narrow range of mind, and proclivity to dominance emerge in her jaw, brow, and shoulders, which project her
authority and power to, paradoxically, the point of a calculated physical attraction. She is someone not of conspicuous intelligence or cul-
ture, but rather clever in managing others, and so keeping them
"under her control." All of this—her physical characteristics, her insistence upon dominance, her categorical indifference to Jane, are a fictional reworking of Charlotte's powerfully antagonistic responses to
Mrs. Sidgwick. For the thin, short, plain Jane—as for Brontë who was
physically just like her—Mrs. Reed made a formidable adversary.

Charlotte left the Sidgewicks on July 13, 1839, but by the end of the
year she writes that she will probably have to take another situation
even though, as she insists, ". . . I *hate* and *abhor* the very thoughts
of governess-ship."

This prediction turned out to be accurate. Early in 1841 she
arrived at Upperwood House, Rawdon, to care for two quite young

children of the White family. As nursery governess caring for small children, Charlotte faced never-ending calls upon her time and attention—demands she had never faced before. Unsurprisingly her letters were soon full of laments. She complains the children are "wild and unbroken." She found it impossible to fit comfortably into family life, wishing to "repel the rude familiarity of the children" while at the same time finding it difficult "to ask either servant or mistress for anything I want." Soon she again found herself in angry opposition to a powerful older woman. She acknowledges in a letter that she's been able to tolerate Mrs. White's bad manners and boastfulness and even her lack of education—demonstrated in her inability to write and spell correctly. But "I have had experience of one little trait in her character which condemns her a long way with me— . . . If any little thing goes wrong she does not scruple to give way to anger in a very coarse unlady-like manner . . . [that] is highly offensive." By August playing the role of governess is becoming insupportable: "it is the living in other people's houses—the estrangement from one's real character—the adoption of a cold, rigid, apathetic exterior, that is painful . . . " Charlotte left the Whites in December but more amicably than her separation from the Sidgwicks, with expressions of gratitude on both sides.

Charlotte Brontë's unsuccessful efforts to find herself a suitable "situation" continued. In February of 1842, just a couple of months after leaving the Whites, Charlotte and her sister Emily traveled to Brussels to study French. At ages twenty-five and twenty-four, they were considerably older than the other pupils, native speakers of French. Charlotte characterized them to Ellen Nussey as "singularly cold, selfish, animal and inferior . . . their principles are rotten to the core." This Yorkshire Protestant found the young Roman Catholic Belgians immediately antipathetic. Nevertheless, by August Madame Heger was sufficiently impressed by this strange pair of young women from Yorkshire to persuade them to stay on at the school as part-time teachers of English and music as well as continue their studies in French to the end of the year.

This return to the role of teacher became the basis for Charlotte's first novel, *The Professor*, which she wrote upon her return to England. Rather than telling this story from her own, female, perspective, Brontë adopted a first-person male narrator named Crimsworth. For many years, she had written in the voice of a male narrator in the fantasy fictions about Angria that she shared with her brother Branwell, so this strategy of adopting a man's perspective was nothing new for her. This narrator, Crimsworth, just like Charlotte, leaves England to teach in Brussels. Like Agnes Grey and the future Jane Eyre, he is at first excited about his new life. "Liberty," he says anticipating Jane's later desire, "I clasped in my arms for the first time and her smile and embrace revived my life." All too soon, however, he finds himself shocked by his female students. Though they are supposedly reared "in utter unconsciousness of vice," these girls take on an "air of bold, imprudent flirtation" with their male teacher, and he soon comes to the conclusion that "the root of this precocious impurity . . . is to be found in the discipline, if not the doctrines of the Church of Rome." His assessment: "the mass of them [were] mentally depraved."

A similarly flawed character with a European and Catholic background appears in *Jane Eyre*, again in an intriguing transposition. When Jane takes up her role as governess, she describes her new pupil, Adèle, a child of seven or eight years, chatting freely in

French but "disinclined to apply" herself to her studies since she had not been systematically educated. Asked about her parents, she recalls her mother taught her "to dance and sing, and to say verse." She recalls parties in which "[a] great many gentlemen and ladies came to see mamma, and I used to dance before them, or to sit on their knees and sing to them." Jane accepts Adèle's offer to perform, and "folding her little hands demurely before her, shaking back her curls, and lifting her eyes to the ceiling she commenced singing a song from some opera. It was the strain of a forsaken lady, who, after bewailing the perfidy of her lover, calls pride to her aid." Jane observes, "The subject seemed strangely chosen for an infant singer; but I suppose the point of the exhibition lay in hearing notes of love and jealousy warbled with the lisp of childhood; and in very bad taste that point was: at least I though so." "Rotten to the core" was the judgment Brontë made of her fellow female students in Brussels, and she clearly intends Adèle to represent yet another victim of continental decadence. As Mr. Rochester is later to put it, feeling sympathy for the destitute child of his French lover, he "took the poor thing out of the slime and mud of Paris" hoping to save her "to grow up clean in the wholesome soil of an English country garden." The scene which the child recalls is indeed prurient. The little girl asked to sit on the knees of her mother's adult male callers and sing songs of perfidy in love, trained—we see this in the folded hands, the tossed curls—to exploit the *frisson* of a sexualized child performing within the context of a morally corrupt Parisian setting. Charlotte Brontë's righteous Protestantism rings loud and clear in this scene, and the challenge for Jane as governess is going to be not so much the obstreperous resistance of Agnes Grey's writhing pupil Tom and his pen knife or Charlotte's demanding charges at Stonegappe as it will be to somehow lead Adèle toward a healthier and more natural childhood; or, as Jane's advertisement phrased it, "a good English education."

Before leaving for Thornfield, Jane Eyre admits to "a private fear," that she is running the risk of something she cannot openly mention. All she can do is hope that "the result of my endeavours" as a new governess will be "respectable, proper, *en règle*." Her anxiety is based upon a very real threat. Typically, a Victorian governess was an educated young woman who came from the same middle-class social rank as members of the family but lacked money. While house servants were not safe from the male sexual predators in a family, the governess, thanks to her class and relative poverty, was in particular danger. On the other hand, unmarried—or even married—men in the family might become so taken by the attractions of a governess as to offer marriage. William Makepeace Thackeray's *Vanity Fair,* which was appearing monthly as Brontë wrote *Jane Eyre,* satirically presents exactly these issues as Becky Sharp flirts with and fends off both Sir Pitt Crawley and his son Rawdon.

During her time as a governess, Charlotte had written to friends about the dominant men in both the families she served. Of the first she told her sister Emily that on a particularily pleasant afternoon she followed after Mr. Sidgwick on a stroll with his children and found herself admiring him: "with his magnificent Newfoundland dog at his side, he looked very like what a frank, wealthy, Conservative gentleman ought to be." Of the family at Upperwood House, she noted to Ellen Nussey, "I like Mr White extremely—respecting Mrs White I am for the present silent—I am trying hard to like her." As we have noted before, and will discuss at length in Chapter Seven, she was soon to fall dangerously in love with Madame Heger's husband in Brussels. For all of her taut observations of and anger at the women of these establishments, Charlotte Brontë clearly felt strong sexual attraction toward the men. Her vivid erotic imagination is evident in the fantasy narratives she had been writing since early adolescence, and she was herself, evidently, always on the lookout for her own opportunities. Jane Eyre, too, setting out to be a governess, is haunted by the erotic possibilities that lie ahead, to which she primly, and frequently, alludes.

On the first morning as her meeting with Adèle, when Mrs. Fairfax makes reference to a Mr. Rochester, Jane is frankly astonished. Mrs. Fairfax is only the "manager." Thornfield has a master.

The truth is out. The comforting hopes for a quiet life are ended. The situation is more complicated than she first expected. Jane is in for some kind of "scrape!"

6

The Master

*J*ane Eyre is a novel about, among other things, mutually shared, passionate love, something Charlotte Brontë had not yet experienced when she wrote the book. Indeed, she had little opportunity to even observe this kind of a relationship, having grown up in a relatively isolated home with her father a widower and her maternal aunt a spinster. And yet the romance between Mr. Rochester and Jane is one of Brontë's greatest achievements as a writer of fiction. How did she do it?

In the pages that follow, we will explore some of the ways that Brontë drew upon her relationships to five men, including two fictional characters, who were central to her emotional life.

Fairfax Rochester himself suggests whom Brontë drew from when inventing his character, in another of those casually presented offhand moments when she obliquely and yet intentionally implies how intimately personal almost all the novel is to her. During one of his first conversations with Jane Eyre, he tries to analyze, in a sexually suggestive moment, why she is reserved and cautious with him. He thinks that she is too fearful to be herself—"to smile too gaily, speak too freely . . . in the presence of a man and a brother—or father, or master, or what you will . . . " Significantly, Mr. Rochester embodies aspects of each one of these persons, and, in weaving them together, Brontë creates her own romantic hero.

For Jane and Rochester's first encounter, Brontë evokes a twilight evening in January. Picturing is always crucial to her art, and here every detail tells us something. The earth is frozen still: solitary, leafless. The chill, the silence suggesting Jane's frozen emotional life.

She is briskly walking the two miles from Thornfield to the nearby town of Hay to post a letter. It's the sort of evening—the sort of errand—that's very familiar to Charlotte Brontë, the "soft, grave" world of her actual experience.

Then Brontë's imagination takes over. The absolute hush is violated by rude noise, a "tramp, tramp; a metallic clatter," and the young Jane sees through the dim light an approaching horse and large dog. She thinks at once of the Gytrash, a frightful creature, sometimes lion-like, which haunted rural roads in Yorkshire legend. Jane's servant nurse Bessie had told stories of this North of England spirit sometimes malevolent, sometimes benevolent, accosting solitary wanderers in the nighttime woods. It's a prodigy and an omen, and also just a dog. It's Rochester's harbinger.

What Charlotte Brontë introduces is nothing less than the composite fulfillment of her own complex and often deeply unhappy secret history of longing and of love. As she often does in this novel, Brontë writes Rochester and his first meeting with Jane to be strikingly different from conventional expectations. In a deliberately antiheroic moment, his horse has just slipped and fallen on the ice, one of Rochester's legs has been injured, and he finds himself forced to ask this plain, small woman he's met in the half-light for help capturing his horse's bridle. Jane reassures the reader that had Rochester been the typically handsome, heroic-looking young gentleman, she would not have known how to reply to his initial, gruff questions. She knew instinctively that such a man would not have had any "sympathy with anything in me . . ." That term—sympathy—is crucial. From this first moment she establishes that there is an equivalence between her and this stranger that she senses instinctively. She further emphasizes it with the language she uses to describe Rochester: he "had a dark face, with stern features and a heavy brow; his eyes and gathered eyebrows looked ireful and thwarted just now . . . " The giveaway, elegantly managed by Brontë, is "ireful"—suggesting the already sensed sympathy between the two. Overhead the moon rises, the symbolic presence of Miss Temple and Bronte's ideal of protective motherhood lighting the scene, watching over Jane Eyre.

Everything about the man—who, fallen from his horse, makes her useful by laying "a heavy hand" on her shoulder—everything comes from Charlotte Brontë's past experience of strong-willed, dominating men who attract her because they are her rivals in one way or another, who exercise an authority over her that she only accepts because there is a kinship bond, a sympathy, between them, and who also paradoxically need her help; men who are physically tough, abrupt, and commanding, powerfully sexualized and dependent on her. Here, distilled into this one man and this one moment, they lean upon her, limping, and then, having caught the bridle of the tall steed, "he mastered it directly." The verb is key. He has regained control, as is chillingly clear in his next command:

"Just hand me my whip,"—which she promptly obeys.

The master but at her mercy. The dominance, and the threat of pain to come—that she is ready to accept. This is the germinal moment of the novel's love story. Unconventional, dangerous, and alluring. Already, Jane has an instinctive sense of the connection few other people would understand. Already, Rochester's pretense of dominance over Jane has been established as a key feature of their relationship. This point is further driven home when finally Jane reenters Thornfield Hall and finds Rochester's silent Newfoundland dog Pilot, which answers to her caress, and learns from a servant "He came with master." Not even "the" here; just "master." The term is twice more repeated in this brief conversation. The reader feels that everything has changed for Jane. Less obvious is the significance of Rochester's arrival for Charlotte. In ways far larger and more complex than in her earlier creation of Helen Burns, she is about to bring out of the shadows of her past—often a very private and secret past—the specter of her desire, and through the evocative power of her imagination make him live.

Charlotte Bronte had observed Rochester's physical vigor, determined will, passionate temper, and defiant courage since the earliest days of her childhood in her father Patrick Brontë. He readily became her first source for the novel's hero.

In Elizabeth Gaskell's biography of Charlotte, she depicts Mr. Brontë as physically vigorous even in middle age, a man of "strong, passionate, Irish nature . . . compressed down with resolute stoicism." A fearless man who took whatever side in local or national politics appeared to him "right." After making enemies of the machine-wrecking Luddites of Haworth when he sided against them in their bitter quarrel with factory owners, and so made enemies of them, he acquired the habit of carrying a loaded pistol. He kept it on his dressing-table with his watch. Ellen Nussey, recalling her first visit to the parsonage during July–August 1833, remembered uneasily that every morning she heard him firing the pistol from his room window, discharging the loading that he made every night. The first edition of Gaskell's biography continues that as a younger man, when angered he would work off his "volcanic wrath" by firing pistols out the backdoor in rapid succession. Lying in bed upstairs, his wife would hear the quick explosions, and know that something was wrong. Soon after Jane Eyre's arrival, she is to learn that Mr. Rochester too has bursts of volcanic wrath, and that when he found his Parisian mistress cheating on him with another man, he called him out for a meeting in the Bois de Boulogne, where he leaves a bullet "in one of his poor etiolated arms." Earlier in his life, trapped on a Caribbean island, driven half-mad by the shrieks of his raving wife, Rochester was to unlock a trunk containing a brace of pistols, preparing to shoot himself in "exquisite and unalloyed despair." He knew Patrick Brontë's rage.

Ellen recalls that Charlotte used to relate the story of a mutilated dress as strong proof of her father's "iron will." Patrick objected to one of his wife's dresses, which had been given to her as a present by someone else. To protect her from "'feminine' temptation," he cut it into shreds. Nussey too sees this as illustrative of Patrick's "will, which ran itself into tyranny and cruelty." The first edition of Gaskell's biography also tells of a nurse setting out "some colored boots" for the children on a rainy day while they were outside. Patrick burned them all thinking they were "too gay and luxurious" and would foster a love of dress. These stories of the dress and the boots, and elements of some of the other tales popularized by Gaskell's first edition, which appeared March 27, 1857, were subsequently challenged by Patrick's denials, the testimony of former house servants Martha Brown and Nancy Garrs, and a series of articles written by local author and friend of the family William Dearden, which appeared in the *Bradford Observer* shortly after the book's publication. Such objections caused Gaskell to revise her text twice. The third edition—what we find now in most reprints—came out in August 1857. Significantly, Mary Taylor, one of Charlotte's oldest and closest friends, wrote this telling assessment: "As to the mutilated" third edition, "I am sorry for it. Libelous or not, the first edition was all true." That term, "true," so crucial to Charlotte Brontë, rings clear in Taylor's judgment. Memory, as we all know, plays strange games with us. In this case the memories of different house servants about events that had occurred decades earlier are in dubious contention. Mary Taylor would have none of it: Gaskell's first version "was all true." What remains is the picture of—as Patrick Brontë himself acknowledged—a somewhat eccentric, highly individual man insistent on going his own way. Nussey sums up Charlotte's father as man of few "sympathies," who in considering an issue never entered into details, who found feelings to be a weakness. Instead, he ruled his opinions by maxims that made "no allowance for idiosyncrasies." In his rough-hewn independence of mind, self-reliant autocracy, and brisk maintenance of his views, Patrick served as a striking model for Charlotte's Fairfax Rochester who will issue judgments and commands to Jane Eyre with rarely a pause to consider her views on an issue.

For the family at Haworth, Patrick was the master. Too poor to ride his own horse, he still had his pistol, pictures of famous battle scenes on the walls of his study, and a commanding presence not only at home but also in his church and in the many community meetings where he fearlessly argued his point of view on matters of often intense and divided interest. In her letters Charlotte always revered her father for his religious faith and devotion, for his learning, and for his tenderness to his children. In the late 1830s and early 1840s, she became more and more dissatisfied with life at home and felt, like Jane Eyre, an inner restlessness, but still she stayed there, nursing her father—just as Jane does Rochester—taking on domestic responsibilities. It was only after *Jane Eyre* had been published, and received largely glowing reviews from the London press, that she told her father of the book's existence. This quiet and respectful subservience to a powerfully dominant man, which Charlotte learned as a child in Patrick Brontë's house, would recur in her later relationships with men both real and imagined. So when Rochester demands the whip, Jane finds it for him.

One aspect of this Church of England clergyman, which Victorian biographers and essayists sometimes pass over in discrete silence, is the fact that he sired six children in little more than six years. While Patrick may have been a bit of a hypochondriac, wrapping his neck in swathes of linen to keep out the cold and eating alone to calm his stomach from the risk of dyspepsia, he had a formidable sex drive. After the tragic and early death of his wife, he proposed in rapid succession to three women all of whom turned him down. It was only then that he settled into the vigorous widower who walked the moors alone. The abrupt, commanding man Jane Eyre encounters in the twilight, whose face she keeps thinking about "because it was masculine . . . dark, strong, and stern," radiates a sexual energy Charlotte Brontë knew, daily, at Haworth.

The well-known photograph of Patrick Brontë, taken in his later years, shows us a gaunt profile with high cheek bones, white hair ruffled like that of a bantam cock, his narrowed eyes peering through his eyeglasses, back still rigidly straight, his mouth pursed and pulled down. He died in 1861 in his eighty-fourth year. His wife and all of his children had died years earlier.

⁓

Charlotte's brother Branwell constitutes a far more complex influence, as well as a second source, for Mr. Rochester. On the face of it, a very unlikely one, too. How could a short, nearsighted, skinny, red-haired kid be transformed into Fairfax Rochester? The explanation is strange but crucial for understanding Charlotte and her novel, and reveals much about the way in which Brontë's imagination worked. From lively younger brother to demonic outlaw, to shattered, self-destroying family humiliation—we will now trace the arc of tragic descent in the life of a man she loved and, in dramatically changing ways, depicted in her fictions.

He was born just over a year after Charlotte (June 1817) and was the constant playmate of his sisters during their childhood. He was, in the biographer Winifred Gérin's sympathetic characterization, "passionate and uncontrolled, violent in nursery games, but so inventive in his willfulness, so avid a reader, so quick a learner," that Charlotte soon recognized him as her mental equal. While their father Patrick was the austere figurehead of the family, in Branwell Charlotte found a kind of fellowship rare in human experience, and she soon transferred to him "the heart's allegiance," once dedicated to her older sister Maria. Her need to love was compelling, and she made him "the focal point of her existence." Together, through their shared writing of poetry and fiction, they created and lived in a world of their own making; note Gérin's term "willfulness." It was to become a key issue in Branwell's relationship with his masterful father—and with his sister—just as "willfulness" was to create, for Jane and Rochester, a climactic crisis in their shared lives.

What began in play quickly evolved into a serious obsession. Charlotte and Branwell created a complex fantasy world, inventing its geography and history and writing the narratives of its principal figures. It's impossible to exaggerate the intimacy of this relationship between sister and brother. They translated their feelings, desires, hopes and dreams into characters, reading and responding to each other's writing, frequently on a daily basis. From early on, Branwell's writing featured the cult of toughness, of aggression, and his heroes soon acquired many of the traits we find in Mr. Rochester, including his powerful sexuality. Perhaps not surprisingly, in this highly unusual sharing of imagination between siblings, questions of dominance soon emerged. Writing, for them, could be a kind of game, in which each sought "to outdo or outmaneuver the other." If we ask, where did the testing banter between Jane Eyre and Mr. Rochester come from, in which they tweak each other's sensibilities, teasing in a love-rivalry, we need look no further—the basis is Charlotte's early adolescent love for and rivalry with her brother. So, in one of many instances, Jane confides to her reader: "I knew the pleasure of vexing" Mr. Rochester, and it is "on the extreme brink I liked well to try my skill." In this kind of play, she tells us, she could still meet him in argument "without fear or uneasy restraint." This kind of relationship "suited both him and me." In this moment of reflection, Charlotte seems to recall the happy years at Haworth when she and Branwell wrote together. Let us have the pleasure of glimpsing their fencing.

This kind of fun is self-evident, for example, in a riposte to a yet earlier piece by Charlotte that begins with Branwell's attack on *her* narrator, Wellsly, as typical of those unprincipled wretches who spend their days "spitting their venom on every author of Reputation within their reach" and "like vipers can do no more than bite the heels of their Enimies." With typical fraternal bravado—and bad spelling—Branwell exults in putting down his sister as an unprincipled wretch, knowing this will provoke her to sit down and begin writing a reply. Like Jane, they both enjoyed playing "on the brink."

Charlotte was ready to return the favor by depicting her brother—here named "Rhymer"—at work, in a script dated July 3, 1830. It opens with comic stage directions: "Rhymer alone in a garret . . . surrounded by shreds of paper and a few old books. Time: half past 11 at night." In this parody version of the Romantic writer she then has him give melodramatic voice. "How solitary is the scene! How sublime likewise!" cries Rhymer. He insists first, for himself, that "from the grave of genius shall arise a fixed star ascending to the heaven of literature . . . to all eternity." Speaking in pseudo-Elizabethan orotundity and employing hackneyed images, this caricature of Branwell's assumption of grandeur claims for himself the immortality of greatness which is the dream and goal of both these young writers. Surely this too was soon passed around the table.

Four years later, in October of 1834 (Charlotte is now eighteen, Branwell seventeen), we find another of Charlotte's comic portraits of Branwell, now satirically depicted as Patrick Benjamin Wiggins. Already there are some important new aspects emerging. Charlotte's male narrator Wellesley spies an indistinct figure in the distance: a short, slight man in a black coat and raven gray trousers, his hat placed nearly at the back of his head, revealing "a bush of carroty hair" his spectacles placed across "a prominent Roman nose," with a black neckerchief carelessly knotted, and, to complete the picture, a little black rattan flourished in his hand. This is a quite exact description of Branwell, who was short; wore eyeglasses; flattered himself in his dress; and had bright, red, curly hair.

Wiggins and the narrator Wellesley walk together to a place very like Haworth, here only slightly renamed "Howard," rather ruthlessly characterized as "a miserable little village" buried in dreary moors and marshes. The lure of the pub draws Wiggins. He emerges boasting that he has guzzled two bottles of "Sneachie's Glass-Town ale" and a double quart of porter, while devouring cheese, bread, and cold beef. "'That,' he boasts, 'is what I call doing the thing in a handsome way!'" Charlotte is alluding to Branwell's adolescent fascination with drink and excess. As they walk Wiggins/Branwell lists his abilities. "As a musician he was greater than Bach; as a poet he surpassed Byron; as a painter, Claude Lorrain yielded to him . . . " and he goes on claiming to also be a rebel; merchant; mill-owner; traveler; the founder of new cities, introducing through them "the arts and the sciences"; and so on.

Charlotte's mocking portrait of her adolescent brother reflects Branwell's role within the family. As the only son, he was to anticipate greatness, and his father clearly favored him. In this sense he was the master in waiting. For example, though his three sisters all drew and painted, it was only Branwell who was sent to train with a professional artist. As they all grew older, it was Branwell who submitted poems and prose to *Blackwell's*, accompanying them with boastful letters about his importance as a writer; and, in later years, he actually had some pieces published in local newspapers. Beneath Charlotte's teasing here we sense her jealous rivalry as well as her mockery of what had become Branwell's bragging assumption that he was on the way to being famous. At this point, much of this seems quite remote from Fairfax Rochester. But not for long.

After Charlotte's Wiggins piece more than five years pass.

Branwell is now twenty-one and a half years old. Charlotte has taught at Roe Head and finally returned home, staggered by bouts of severe depression. Branwell continues to write prolifically. He has tried out a career as a portrait painter and failed. Their relationship has changed. In Charlotte's long, two-part novella *Henry Hastings,* written in 1839, her ironic comic treatment of her brother has now disappeared. The cynical narrator of the piece is her favorite male stand-in, now renamed Charles Townshend. Captain Henry Hastings is Branwell. Elizabeth Hastings, his sister, closely resembles Charlotte and is a prototype of Jane Eyre. The narrative chronicles Henry Hasting's degradation and his sister's involvement in his ruin.

What has caused this dramatic alteration in the way Charlotte writes about her brother? What has happened to Benjamin Patrick Wiggins? And in what ways has this depiction moved far closer to the Mr. Rochester of Jane's first encounters with him at Thornfield Hall?

The years 1834 to 1839 span a dramatic shift in the relationship, influenced by the fact that Branwell, between the ages of seventeen and twenty-two, becomes more independent of family dominance and control, while Charlotte, between eighteen and twenty-three, enters into an emotional and psychological crisis. Necessarily, they are growing up, and for both of them this proved a very difficult process.

Here we note just a few of the crucial changes taking place. When Charlotte leaves for Roe Head, Branwell's stories take on a rebelliousness that pushes the edges of what had been permissible in Patrick Brontë's parsonage. In the spring of 1834, he writes a long biography of his new Angrian hero Alexander Percy. He describes Percy as a slender but active boy with "eminently handsome features." Clearly this is a stand-in for himself. And then, a note of perhaps consciously anticipated danger: like Branwell, Percy is given to "tumultuous passions" with a mind "totally destitute of religious restraint or moral principle." Puberty drives much of this, legitimating the writer's own growing independence of mind and of conduct. The bold rejection of both religion and conventional morality coming from the son of a stern and commanding clergyman father asserts a rebellion that, at least at this point in his life, Branwell was happy to conceal in writings his father did not read.

Though the siblings were no longer together at Haworth, by the end of this same year, Charlotte is undergoing similar changes, flirting with the unthinkable, as we find in her warning her friend Ellen not to read texts that must have been at that time familiar to Charlotte: Byron's *Don Juan* and *Cain*. Charlotte too is exploring rebellion and dissent. She too is playing with danger.

While Charlotte found herself trapped at Roe Head, Branwell more and more indulged his enthusiasm for boxing, gathering with chums in local pubs to scan the sporting news and cheer on local champs. Drinking—often to excess—was a part of these liberating masculine pleasures.

Then, in early November 1836, Branwell kills off a major character in the middle of a continuing, episodic narrative titled "Angria and the Angrians": Mary Percy, one of Charlotte's great favorites in whom she invested much of her emotional connection to the Angrian story. To most people this would simply seem to be the latest move in their shared play. To Charlotte it was a crisis. Her shock at this death was intensified by how Branwell describes Mary Percy's last hours. He openly rejects the usual, saccharine spiritual elements of the deathbed scene. There is to be no "mingling of Heaven with earth," nothing of that "Angelic hope" of life after death. Instead this is to be "the end of a Child of earth," a woman whose soul and spirit were "rooted in earth" and in dying cries out at what is happening to her as she is "being torn away from it." Branwell had been inclined—more insistently as time passed—to doubt the religious consolations for death that were central to his father's life and indeed his father's profession. In this moment a character Charlotte saw as an extension of herself abandons expectations of heavenly consolation and speaks in despair, voicing her anguish at being separated from her great love. This is what makes death so "terrible" for her.

Mary Percy voices Branwell's own darkening vision and, though it is perhaps not the intention of her creator, of Charlotte as well. Charlotte was plunging deeper into her own, parallel, spiritual crisis. In December, just a month later, she writes to Ellen Nussey, "I know not how to pray." She despairs of living what she considers a life of "doing good" and instead sees herself as "seeking my own pleasure," the "Gratification of my own desires." In this, she confesses that she has forgotten God and voices the anxious fear, "will not God forget me?" It is as if the Mary Percy written by Branwell has spoken for Charlotte in her tormented devotion to things earthly, the flesh, pleasure, "my own desires." What Charlotte can plausibly mean by these generalities is hard to imagine given the strictly controlled character of her daily life. But the desperation and guilt are there nonetheless, dramatically voiced.

The correspondence of thinking between brother and sister did not, as one might expect, evoke a sympathetic sense of shared crisis, and for a simple reason. Charlotte chose repression and silence—save for the odd letter to her friend—and the hope of self-discipline. Whereas Branwell, in the ensuing months, chose risk-taking, excess, the pursuit of "the earth." Readers of *Jane Eyre* will immediately recall Rochester's narration of his years of wandering through Europe in which he claims to have "tried dissipation" but never yields to "debauchery," a distinction that may escape the more skeptical reader. And we should note here too the first hints of what is later to become a crucial debate between Jane and Rochester at a climactic moment in the novel, when he begs, cajoles, and virtually commands, threatening—"I'll try violence," he says—her to choose a life of fleshly pleasure by living in a bigamous sexual relationship with him in an ironically pictured "white-washed villa" on the shores of the Mediterranean. Of course, she refuses.

Now we see the crucial differences taking clear form. Rochester is stopped from plunging "headlong into wild license" only by Jane's resistance. Branwell, in the late 1830s, was becoming just that man. First in his writing of fantasy chronicles. A bit later, in his own, actual life. And his sister Charlotte found herself powerless to do anything about it.

By October of 1837 in Branwell's "Angria and the Angrians" we find an example of this development in the blasphemous, drunken toast he writes for Henry Hastings.

"Its speedy entombment in our stomachs and its ressurection with us in another world!"

The President himself contradicted such a toast swearing that He had enough to do with . . . resurrection of its ghost next morning and Crofton vowed that after a full dinner and flowing glass he had too often been troubled with its resurrection the next minute.

Branwell thus enjoys mocking the central tenant of Christianity, the resurrection of Jesus, which he transforms into a joke having to do with hangovers and vomiting. Presumably it was the kind of ribaldry Branwell indulged in when he met his drinking buddies at the Black Bull, down the hill from the Haworth parsonage. In the next few years, Branwell continued to write about what Juliet Barker terms "the unfortunate Henry Hastings" and the vicious circle of his debauched friends.

When Charlotte, finally liberated from teaching at Miss Wooler's school in February of 1839, took up a new writing project, she chose as its title the name of Branwell's dissipated spokesman, a character he had been writing about since December of 1834. Into this project she poured her complicated feelings toward her brother and what was now happening to him. Hastings, as the story opens, is running from the law, and Charlotte describes him in ways that anticipate Rochester. There are, first, the handsome, yet dark, demonic looks. While he is a man of a muscular and powerful frame, he isn't tall, and he has "a worn and haggard aspect" even though he is still young. His looks reflect the life he has been living and what has happened to his spirit. The narrator, judging by the man's face, concludes, "he must have been blessed with a devil's temper. I never saw such a mad, suspicious irritability as glinted in his little black eyes." Much of this cannot literally be Branwell—who was slender and not of a powerful frame and red not dark haired. But as we see, both Charlotte and Branwell reveled in the adoption of fictional personae, and so in writing about Hastings Charlotte writes about one of her brother's stand-in figures. And her presentation of this character is dramatically negative. But how have his eyes become irritable and mad; how has Branwell's former good nature morphed into a "habitual scowl"?

The story characterizes Henry Hastings as a traitor who has "blotted out his family name with stains of infamy." Though probably a man under thirty, "strong drink and bad courses had ploughed lines in his face which might better have suited three score." Charlotte is working out what has happened to her younger brother. She depicts Hastings—as Branwell—with passions "naturally strong" and with a feverous imagination. The two together make "wild work," especially when "drunken delirium lashed them up . . . He was talked of everywhere for his excesses." There is a tragic and prescient vision at play in this crucial passage. Branwell's sister is castigating him for his youthful delight in tavern fun with his pals and his failure, so far, to achieve the success and consequent recognition that he claimed for his genius. She is also, unfortunately, accurately anticipating what was to happen. Branwell's strong passions and lively imagination, his propensity for "excesses," those very elements that could make him so charming and fun in company, which made him a fellow writer of such energy and vision, could lead him to waste his vigor and his youth in vice, and her story was meant as a cautionary tale, a warning about what is ahead unless he alters his conduct. For Charlotte as the eldest sister, a crucial aspect is the danger that he could stain his family name with "infamy."

In all of this we see hints at the future emergence of Mr. Rochester—his mistaken marriage to Bertha Mason, whose own bestiality takes to its logical limits Rochester's own animal propensities, his subsequent life of debauchery in Paris, and his saturnine good looks reflecting his previous excesses and suffering. Strangely, one might think almost perversely, Charlotte is transforming her brother into a Byronic hero, ally to Satan, making the great refusal. And in Branwell's writing—the blasphemous toast, Mary Percy's deathbed scene, and much of his later poetry and prose—we see how the younger brother has prepared the way for this. For the son of a disciplined and faithful parish priest, a stain indeed. Thinking, writing, even conduct in rebellion against the mastery of his father, as if in a frantic effort to supplant it. The years subsequent to the writing of *Henry Hastings* were to prove its tragic foresight, and Charlotte's growing indignation with her brother's conduct was to lead to the total breakdown of their friendship and her cold refusal to sympathize with his decline or to endeavor in any substantive way to save him from himself. Instead he was to emerge in the ominous earlier experiences of Fairfax Rochester, and Brontë was to "save" the brother—who had become so much like Hastings—through Jane Eyre's redemption of the novel's male hero.

In *Henry Hastings* we find Charlotte too—and as well an anticipation of Jane Eyre—in the story's portrayal of Henry's sister Elizabeth. Charlotte paints a decidedly unglamorous portrait of her as an "insignificant, unattractive" young woman wholly without the bloom, majesty, or fullness of beauty. Her simplicity of appearance is matched by her self-repression: her features seem masked, her physical movements restrained and guarded. She lacks "openness, originality, frankness." Elizabeth Hastings comes from a rough, wild country of moors and mountains with hardly any green fields, no trees, and stony, bad roads. In all of this we read a diminished and disempowered Charlotte writing herself into the story of her brother's transformed and darkened life. Like Charlotte, and indeed like Jane Eyre to come, Elizabeth struggles to keep wrapped about her the "veil of reserve and propriety" at moments of crisis, when incidents of strange excitement were transpiring around her on the point of bursting forth like lava. Here the contrast between sister and brother is explicit. Two who were so close are now facing an unbridgeable divide.

On July 31, 1845, Charlotte returned home from a short trip to find Branwell in a terrible state: in a letter to Ellen Nussey she writes that he had received a note from his employer Mr. Robinson sternly dismissing him and intimating that he had discovered that Branwell was engaging in conduct that he characterized as "bad beyond expression" and charged him, on pain of exposure, to sever any connection with his family. Charlotte in her letter tries to decorously skirt the particulars—Branwell had embarked on an adulterous love affair with Mr.—actually Reverend—Robinson's wife, and they had been caught. Now Charlotte and the rest of the family had to deal with the results: "he thought of nothing but stunning, or drowning his distress of mind." Ultimately they had to send him away from the parsonage for a week. Branwell had been boasting for years about his ways with the ladies. Sexual energy is an important aspect of the master. Now, having been caught and repulsed, he turned at once to drink—"drowning"—and probably opium—"stunning." He will not listen and he will not change. The fearful dismay Charlotte feels and writes about was exactly replicated in *Jane Eyre*. When Jane refuses Rochester's anguished plea that they ignore religious and legal barriers and flee to the south of France, she knows she must get away from his anger and from his threats of physical coercion. But she fears what he will do to himself. She dreads being an "instrument of evil" to him, anticipating that he might fling himself into the same self-destructive debauchery Charlotte witnessed in the life of her brother.

By January 30, 1846, she writes of Branwell that he never even attempted to find a new job and that he had reached the point where no one will hire him. This is not the worst of it; if he had any money "he would use it only to his own injury." While *Henry Hastings* depicts Branwell-as-Hastings worn and scarred by excess, he is still clear-headed, active, and struggling against his enemies. By 1846 Branwell had tragically become much more like the Bertha Mason of *Jane Eyre* only worse. Whereas Bertha's slide into bestiality is hereditary and unavoidable, Branwell's degeneration was self-chosen and self-willed and could only lead to an early death.

When Charlotte imagined Mr. Rochester, what she pictured was in part the still romantically energetic and mysterious Henry Hastings and not the once delightful brother of her youth whom she now evidently disdainfully considered hopeless. But what fuels much of Rochester's power is the novel's frequent suggestions that in his past and, indeed, his present life he faces similar temptations and through strength of will must master himself and his fate. Or, far more darkly, bend other people and even his "fate" to his willful desire. So, for example, one afternoon, early in their relationship, Jane Eyre finds herself baffled by Mr. Rochester's inexplicable anger and bitterness as he confronts Thornfield's façade. Raising his eye to its battlements, he casts over them a glare of "Pain, shame, ire—impatience, disgust, detestation." The conflict is a struggle between his past and what he might become. Much later the reader and Jane come to understand that he is thinking about his wife locked up in the third floor of the family country estate. Then, "another feeling rose and triumphed: something hard and cynical; self-willed and resolute." It will be his decision to preserve the secret hidden there and to pursue the ignorant and innocent governess now under his spell. This thought "steeled his passion and petrified his countenance." As Rochester's secrets come to light, this scene looks darker and darker, his cruel will more shameless and immoral. Here, and later, he remains in charge, knowing that what he is doing—and willfully choosing to do—is wrong. Having confronted her brother's will to destroy himself—Branwell was all too eager to profess this intention during the final months of his life—Brontë in scenes such as this presents a Rochester willing himself to do what he knows is wrong, a commitment he persists in until the very day of his aborted marriage to Jane Eyre and, indeed, thereafter as he urges her to defy conventional morality and flee south with him. It's only at this point that Jane's will defies him as she deserts him, running away from him much as, in her feelings and in her conduct, Charlotte Brontë was to more sternly defy and reject her pathetic brother in the final, perhaps inexorable, months of his willed self-destruction.

In Chapter Two we have seen Charlotte dreaming about Zamorna during her frustrating years as a teacher at Roe Head, picturing him in the moonlight standing by his war horse listening to "distant wild and wailing music." And from the same period we glanced in Chapter Four at one of her poems celebrating this heroic figure from the Angrian chronicles in idolatrous terms: "He's not the temple but the god . . . for me he dwells divine." More than any other creation of the shared juvenilia, Zamorna was for Charlotte the emotional center of the project—dangerously, immorally attractive, and consequently, at the same time, the cruel yet desperately loved husband of her favorite heroine Mary Percy, whose tragic feelings for him fascinated her. Charlotte and Branwell had been writing about him for more than a decade. So, it is not surprising that, as she began to invent Mr. Rochester, she would draw upon this third source for the shadowy rider emerging from the dusk, and as the ireful master of Thornfield who steels his will to take Jane no matter what the consequences. The challenging thing for Charlotte as she writes *Jane Eyre* is to keep her demonic hero exciting and masterful, and then to somehow tame him into being the better man Rochester dreams Jane can help him become.

In her "A Peep into a Picture Book," which the eighteen-year-old Charlotte dates June 16, 1834, Wellesley, her favorite narrator, is turning the pages and happens upon a portrait of his older brother Zamorna.

Though always prone to criticizing and often deriding Zamorna, a strategy Charlotte frequently uses to keep her rapt fascination with this dangerous hero under control, in these pages Wellesley cannot ignore the man's magnetic physical attraction. "Keen, glorious being!" His good looks are, Wellesley thinks, as sharp and brilliant as the scimitar hanging at his side, an exotic weapon that he whirls with the same delicate hand which grasps the bridle of his horse. The horse and the hands anticipate Mr. Rochester on the night Jane first meets him. Perhaps, too, the eyes, which "bode no good . . . Satan gave them their glory." Spiritual rebellion defines him: "impetuous sin, stormy pride, diving and soaring enthusiasm." This is the youthful Charlotte's hero. We can trace in this passage many of the influences that shaped her as a writer of fiction, and we can see emerging recurrent elements that will reappear twelve years later in Mr. Rochester.

Charlotte and Branwell—like many Romantics—were intoxicated by the romantic reinterpretation of Milton's Satan as the real hero of *Paradise Lost*. Hurled from heaven for his refusal to serve God's mastery, the rebellious Lucifer finds himself in the newly made inferno, where

> . . . the thought
> Both of lost happiness and lasting pain
> Torments him; round he throws his baleful eyes
> That witness'd huge affliction and dismay
> Mixt with obdurate pride and steadfast hate . . .
>
> his face
> Deep scars of Thunder had intrencht, and care
> Sat on his faded cheek, but under Browes

Of dauntless courage, and considerate Pride
Waiting revenge . . .

Crucial to both Milton's Satan and Charlotte's description of
Zamorna—and Rochester—are these eyes, brilliant with defiance.
Her young demon revels in the impetuous sin and stormy pride that
first caused Lucifer to rebel against divine authority. Rochester gaz-
ing up at the battlements of Thornfield Hall, defying his fate, grind-
ing his teeth, stamping on the hard ground, preparing to break
God's law and man's, was to be but the next, most complete of
Brontë's adaptations of this figure.

To Milton's rebellious and fallen angel Charlotte added another
literary character famous in her day, which she also found dramatically appealing, the Byronic hero. Here is Byron's Giaour of 1813
emerging from the darkness:

Who thundering comes on blackest steed,
With slackened bit and hoof of speed?
Beneath the clattering iron's sound
The caverned Echoes wake around . . .

This figure of male power and aggression, the "thundering" of his
steed anticipating the "tramp, tramp" of Mr. Rochester's first
appearance in *Jane Eyre,* has all of Satan's mysterious attractiveness,
defiant rebelliousness, and bitter recollection of the past:

Dark and unearthly is the scowl
That glares beneath his dusky cowl:
The flash of that dilating eye
Reveals too much of times gone by . . .

Oft with his glance the gazer rue,

For in it lurks that nameless spell,

Which speaks, itself unspeakable,

A spirit yet unquelled and high,

That claims and keeps ascendancy . . .

Ascendency is the issue in all these cases. Milton's Satan refuses to accept his defeat even as he acknowledges God's superior power. Byron's Giaour will fail to save the beautiful Leila from Hassan, but he will kill his adversary nonetheless. Rochester has tried to lock up the secret of his past as he defies his fate pursuing the innocent young governess.

Crucial for Byron and for Brontë's heroes, both Zamorna and Rochester, is the stallion, the commanding hands, the reins of mastery. In her poem of December 19, 1835, "We Wove a Web in Childhood," Charlotte elaborated on these elements in depicting Zamorna in an aristocratic setting, which in various ways anticipates Mr. Rochester at Thornfield. One evening Zamorna arrives looking like a "spurred and fur-wrapped demi-god." Soon the erotic emerges as Zamorna finds his chosen one by his side, and

That hand, that in its horseman's glove

Looked fit for naught but bridle rein,

Caresses now its lady-love

With fingers white that show no stain

They got in hot and jarring strife

When hate or honour warred with life . . .

Brontë revels in this conflation of violence and the sensual. There's more than a little suggestion of the pleasures here shared by the

dominating man and the dominated woman. Brontë already anticipates Rochester's whip.

In Charlotte's long story *Caroline Vernon* (1839), the account of
Zamorna's satanic mastery darkens. The title character, in many
ways similar, like Elizabeth Hastings, to her inventor Charlotte
Brontë and hence later to Jane Eyre, is a young woman with a very
ambiguous relationship with a male authority figure: her guardian.
She grows under Zamorna's care into a fine and accomplished girl,
but one who is perhaps too fresh, naïve, and romantic. She longs "to
give up heart, soul, sensations to one adored hero," to lose independent existence in "the perfect adoption of her lover's being." Caroline's ignorant and idealized notions of love echo Charlotte's in at
least one aspect. In a letter written to Ellen Nussey in March of 1839,
only months before the draft of this novella, she tells her close friend
that if she is ever to marry, it can only be to a man for whom her
"intense attachment" would make her "willing to die" for him.

Caroline's romantic ignorance soon emerges as a danger—it's
as if Brontë in thinking about her extravagant notions of absolute
self-abandonment for love has become wary of the inherent dangers in this attitude and wishes to explore them in this fiction.
Once a kind protector, Zamorna comes to desire Caroline, giving
himself over to "propensities that were often stronger than his reason." Brontë intentionally wishes to disturb her reader with the
overt suggestion of incest—a theme she had found dangerously
attractive in Byron's poetry. Later, in writing *Jane Eyre,* she will
constantly stress her heroine's small body, her reclusive passivity,
which, deceptively, make her seem a little Jane to Rochester who
relishes lording it over her.

Caroline now yields to passion. Dressing as a man, she comes to
Zamorna's palace unannounced, driven by "her wild, frantic attach-

ment." The worldly wise narrator warns that as for Zamorna, "all things bright and fair live for him;" and so he feels free, as Rochester is later to do, to take and to use whomever he desires. Caroline "darkly saw, or rather felt" what was happening but is overwhelmed with emotional delirium. Zamorna's magnetic ruthlessness dominates her. His deep voice, dark and burning eyes strike her "with a thrill of nameless dread." This is no longer her guardian; "something terrible sat in his place." Exactly like Rochester after the revelation of Bertha Mason, Zamorna urges Caroline to go away with him. He too has a "little retreat," deceptively looking like "a plain old house outside." There, "nobody will ever reach it to disturb you. It lies on the verge of the moors." At this point Caroline's conscience is too feeble to oppose her passion. Zamorna kisses her saying, "in that voice of fatal sweetness which has instilled venom into many a heart, 'Will you go with me to-morrow, Caroline?'" And her answer is a simple "Yes."

These cross comparisons clearly demonstrate that Charlotte Brontë had been for many years working out characters, situations, and ethical problems she was later to handle so deftly in *Jane Eyre*. Tempted, Caroline Vernon will succumb to Zamorna's amoral seduction as the younger Charlotte Brontë seemed to do in the years when she reveled in escape to her fantasy world depicted in poems describing him as her "god." This yearning vulnerability of a young woman eagerly "throwing her heart and soul into her dreams, longing only for an opportunity to do what she feels she could do" constitutes a kind of self-analysis for Charlotte Brontë at this crucial point in her life. Approaching twenty-four years of age, deeply unhappy in the roles of school teacher and governess, voicelessly yearning much as Jane Eyre was to be upon her arrival at Thornfield, feeling the desperation of time passing, uselessness, the sense that her genius as a writer had foundered and mattered to no one, Charlotte imagined the "wild, devoted enthusiasm" of yielding to the master, a much older, already married, highly sexed man, as a blissful release and fulfillment.

And then it almost seemed as if fate had just that destiny in store for her.

7

Cord of Communion

Of all the secrets in Charlotte Brontë's life, her experiences during the years 1842–1845, including her two-year stay in Brussels, were the most closely held, the most carefully guarded. In various ways she had been able to deal with her feelings for her father, her brother, for the romantic extravaganzas of her fantasy projections. Now, unexpectedly, she found herself plunged into the torment of a love that would become the far more powerful inspiration for much of Jane Eyre's relationship with Mr. Rochester. And the secret of that love, and of what happened because of it, she guarded with jealous hostility from everyone she knew. And yet, again the paradox: in Rochester, more than in any other aspect of *Jane Eyre*, Brontë hid the most important moments of her recent life in full view for all the world to see.

In the years following Charlotte's death, Elizabeth Gaskell, her first biographer, intentionally suppressed what she had learned from a visit to Brussels, which included conversations with the principal people involved and glimpses of a correspondence that was not published until many years later. Winifred Gérin carefully traces Gaskell's efforts in "whitewashing Charlotte" to create a portrait of her as a good and admirable woman, rather than someone passionately in love with a married man. Which is, for all of its oddities of development, the central ethical question in *Jane Eyre*.

Plans for the Brontë sisters to open a school in Haworth led to efforts to find a suitable place for Charlotte and Emily to learn French. Through a local clergyman, an acquaintance of their father's, they learned of a *pensionnat*, a boarding school for girls, in Brussels and of a young English woman studying there who could vouch for its respectability. When the owners learned the Brontës were, as they described themselves, daughters of an English clergyman of moderate means anxious to learn French with a view of instructing others, they offered to accept them at a lower rate, essentially as scholarship students. Everyone involved was actuated by the finest motives.

For Charlotte and Emily, whose lives had been spent in rural parts of Yorkshire, nearly everything about this experience was incredible. Elizabeth Gaskell writes a full two pages simply narrating the hundreds of years of history that lay behind the building housing the school, a place that "had its own ghostly train of splendid associations," which included a Renaissance infanta, an aristocratic guild of crossbow men, the mansion built for their splendid feasts, and the residence of their master-archer. In this shadowy anticipation of Thornfield and its own mysterious history they found themselves, in February of 1842, among eighty to a hundred pupils whose education was administered by a cool, professional woman, Zoë Claire Heger. Gaskell beautifully characterizes the first weeks of the Brontë sisters in this utterly new place: they "clung together" and kept themselves at a distance apart from the happy, boisterous, well-befriended Belgian girls, who, in their turn, thought these new English pupils wild and scared-looking, with "strange, odd, insular ideas about dress."

Their French teacher, from the start, was Mme. Heger's husband: M. Constantin Georges Romain Heger. At the time Charlotte was twenty-five, M. Heger thirty-three, his wife thirty-eight. In an important letter of May 1842 to Ellen Nussey, recording her early days at the pensionnat, Charlotte noted how she enjoyed the new discipline she was experiencing in taking orders from her professor. Having been a schoolteacher and then a governess, she finds it odd and yet strangely pleasing to again obey. She goes on, describing Monsieur Heger, the professor of rhetoric, as a man with a powerful intellect and a choleric temper. Sometimes he borrows the lineaments of "an insane Tom-cat"—sometimes those of a "delirious Hyena." After which, she must generously acknowledge that occasionally—but very seldom—he could be "mild & gentleman-like." However, there are problems: she finds herself troubled because he is very angry at the present moment—she has written a translation that he chooses to stigmatize as less than correct. Childishly, Brontë explains this is the case because he happened to be in "a bad humour" when he read it. Then, she tells her friend Ellen, when "he is very ferocious with me I cry - - & that sets all things straight." Here we get an early glimpse of this new version of the master. It's easy to see in these remarks, in the dominating brusqueness of his manner, in his intellectual authority and command, and in the dark, dramatic looks of her new teacher, the outlines of Mr. Rochester appearing.

There was much to admire in M. Heger. He was, at the time, professor at the Brussels Athénée Royal. He had fought on the barricades in September 1830 for Belgian independence, his first wife's brother dying at his side. That wife and their only child had died of cholera in 1833. He later married Zoë Claire Parent in 1836, and they were to have six children.

In many ways he resembled Patrick Brontë and anticipated Charlotte's projection of him in Mr. Rochester. Constantin, like Patrick, was strong-willed and courageous, a man with a considerable sex drive who knew how to handle a gun, and yet also a tender and thoughtful teacher and father. As a young man he, like Mr. Rochester, had lived in Paris, though for Heger it was to attend the Comédie-Francais, which gave him a zest for dramatic readings of texts. For this daughter of a Cambridge-educated clergyman, Heger's learning was of compelling importance. He was deeply versed in French literature, and as he got to know the Brontë sisters furnished them with books in French and German as well as reprints of his own addresses at the Athénée Royal. Just as Patrick selflessly dedicated himself to the calling of parish priest, Heger regarded teaching as his life's work. Thus when later he became discontented with the secular ideology of the Athéné, he resigned his appointment as principal to teach only the youngest students. He was for many years a member of the Society of Saint Vincent de Paul, visiting and caring for the poor and sick of the city, and gathering working-class people together for evening lectures in which, as one of his local friends wrote, he found "ways to entertain them even while he teaches them." This charitable work overcame Charlotte's lifelong, rabid anti-Catholicism, at least for the moment, and her respect for his care for others, be they pupils or the local poor, is reflected in her letter's characterization of him as gentleman-like, something she found impressive.

Heger quickly recognized that in Charlotte and Emily he had two exceptional students, and he instituted a tutorial for them both in which he had them read French texts he judged exemplary models and then asked them to write "devoirs" on similar topics. A number of these exercises with Heger's corrections and comments survive— Elizabeth Gaskell's biography reprints one, and Sue Lanoff has published all of them in an excellent modern edition. They illustrate in the professor's marginal notes and comments Heger's high standards for clarity of prose and accuracy of argument—an excellent discipline for Charlotte as a writer, which, as her early letter suggests, she coupled with what seems to be an almost masochistic need to—as she puts it—submit to his authority. Jane Eyre, as we will see in Chapter Eight, is equally prepared to submit her school drawings to Mr. Rochester's imperious evaluations.

On November 2 Charlotte and Emily received news in Brussels of the fatal illness of their Aunt Branwell who—quite unlike Jane Eyre's ruthlessly cruel Aunt Reed—had cared for them at home for most of their lives. They hastened to return to Haworth carrying with them a letter to their father from M. Heger voicing his condolences and urging that the sisters return to continue their studies after the period of mourning. He wrote their father of his concern that this sudden separation threatened to destroy the "almost fatherly affection" that he has offered them, and he finds himself pained at the thought of so much work disrupted, "of so many things well begun." His concern is "a matter of affection," and he asks that Patrick Brontë pardon him if he writes of his children, when he discusses their futures, "as if they were a part of our family." He sees their personal qualities, such as their willingness, indeed, their extreme eagerness, to study and to learn, as the reason why he writes in this way. It is intriguing to speculate on how this kind of rhetoric affected Charlotte privately as Heger characterizes himself as a father figure, given her own complex feelings for Patrick Brontë and her

projection of them, as we have seen in Chapter Six, into the dangerous passion she explores in *Caroline Vernon* where a young woman
yields to the aggressive desires of a ruthless man. And so this mag-
netically commanding personality, only eight years Charlotte's
senior, urges their return to complete important work now disrupted.
Unique in her experience, this voicing of a desire that she return to
improve as a writer—that was the central thrust of Heger's training
of both sisters—must have suggested a validation of Charlotte she
had never encountered before. It stands in dramatic contrast to
Southey's reply to her letter of six years earlier, and we can presume
that it made a strong impression on her in light of her subsequent
feelings for Heger.

In the end Emily remained at home. Charlotte returned.

The second year, now lived without her sister, and troubled by
her growing attraction to Heger, proved far more difficult than the
first. Charlotte writes to Ellen Nussey of her life in Brussels, finding
it monotonous, and, far worse, her feeling a constant sense of "solitude in the midst of numbers." And yet she concedes she is thankful to be here, rather than back as governess to Mrs. Sidgwick or
Mrs. White. Sexual issues if anything have become progressively
more prominent. In this same letter she repudiates the gossip she
has heard from England that she is seeking a husband. She notes
that she never exchanges a word with any man other than Monsieur Heger and seldom indeed with him, and then goes on to char-
acterize speculations about a woman who has "neither fortune nor
beauty" desiring to get married as an "imbecility which I reject
with contempt." Instead, she argues, it is wiser for such women to
convince themselves that they are "unattractive" and that they had
better be quiet and think of "other things than wedlock." She seems
to be consciously stifling hope. Charlotte classes herself as a woman

who reasonably cannot expect any man to find her interesting. She must therefore anticipate a life without marriage. The loneliness felt by this English, Protestant girl critically intensified during the summer vacation months when the school was virtually empty of students. Meanwhile the presence of M. Heger as the only man she had a meaningful relationship with made the growing tension within herself all the worse. The letter, while overtly ignoring her emerging passion, hints at the conditions that caused its aching growth.

In the end Charlotte resolved to return to Haworth, despite the urgings of both Hegers, husband and wife, that she remain. On the first day of 1844, M. Heger accompanied her to Ostend, giving her a copy of *Les Fleurs de la Poésie Francais* and a diploma certifying her work at the school. Several weeks later she wrote to her friend Ellen from Haworth describing how much she suffered as she left Brussels, saying she would never forget "what the parting with Mons Heger cost me." It grieved her that in leaving she had grieved him who had been so "true and kind and disinterested a friend"; a complex of regret, guilt, and frustrated desire that would return in Jane Eyre's grief as she flees Mr. Rochester and Thornfield. She continues that she will soon be twenty-eight and ought to be working and "braving the rough realities of the world" as other people do. The interlacing of age, sexual longing, and the unpleasant prospect of future work emerge here, as they will later in *Jane Eyre* as Jane, having fled Mr. Rochester, accommodates to life as teacher in the remote village of Morton.

In the months that followed, Charlotte began writing M. Heger a series of letters in French. There may have been many of them. Significantly, the letters are all addressed to him, personally, and they put him in a difficult position. Only when his answers became rarer, and when they ceased altogether, did she begin to attribute his silence to the intervention of his wife. In reality, as Gérin concludes, "he set no great store by them," and so sooner or later he tore them up. However, Madame diligently collected the torn-up pieces from his basket, stitched, gummed, pasted, and glued them together again. When she did this is not at all clear. Her motive, when she did reconstitute them, must have been, Gérin suggests, that fearing some blemish might attach to her husband in the correspondence with a by then famous author, she preserve them because whatever happened "the integrity of M. Heger as a teacher of young girls must never be called into doubt." Mme. Heger had come to realize that her dubious regard for Charlotte's feelings and motives, which had led to progressively more chilly treatment of this woman from Yorkshire, was amply justified.

In Charlotte's first surviving letter dated July 24, 1844, and so a half year after her return to Haworth, she writes of her hope to visit M. Heger again in Brussels: "it must happen since I so long for it," she insists. She then complains, as if unconsciously transferring her father's growing health crisis to herself, that at the moment her eyesight is too weak for writing—"if I wrote a lot I would become blind." And then she adds, suggesting that Heger is aware of her ambitions, that if she didn't have this fear she would write a book and she would dedicate it "to my literature master— the only master that I have ever had—to you Monsieur." With this, Charlotte articulates in concise terms that their relationship has been unique in her experience and her sense that it is a relationship of master to disciple—a relationship of dominance eagerly accepted as not only correct but also satisfying and pleasurable. Writing and literary achievement emerges from this relationship and the feelings that it impels.

Heger's letters in reply, which have not survived, seem to have contained nothing more than "kindly advice" about her studies and her mode of life.

In the third surviving letter from January 8, 1845, written a whole year after her departure from Brussels, she laments that Heger has not been replying to her letters and though she tries to "master" her feelings, like Caroline Gordon, she suffers from "an almost unbearable inner struggle." She has "tormenting dreams," in which she sees him "always severe, always saturnine and angry with me," and she adds that she refuses to resign herself to the total loss of "my master's friendship." She would prefer to undergo "the greatest bodily pains" rather than have her heart constantly "lacerated by searing regrets." The masochistic character of her feelings for him is clear. She continues, pitifully begging for "a little friendship," professing she does not need "a great deal of affection from those I love" and, indeed, is not accustomed to it but wishes only to preserve the "<u>little</u> interest" he once had in her. It is instructive to compare the language of this letter with the subsequent, imagined relationship between Jane Eyre and her "Master." Mr. Rochester will torment Jane, stage managing an elaborate house party in order to hurt her into loving him, forcing her to "conceal" her feelings and "smother hope." At the end of an evening, he quizzes Jane, seemingly eagerly happy to observe that tears of pain are already "shining and swimming" in her eyes. Yet, while drawing upon these memories as she writes, Brontë is able to foresee a resolution to Jane's suffering, something Charlotte will not permit herself to hope for.

The fourth and final surviving letter dated November 18, 1845, starts by lamenting she has not heard from him for six months. She feels humiliated that she does not know how to gain "mastery over one's own thoughts." She feels herself to be "the slave of a regret, a memory, the slave of a dominant and fixed idea," which, she admits, "has become a tyrant over one's mind." Here her language is even more overt: mastery, slave, dominance, tyrant. Charlotte was very familiar with all of this. Ruthless domination is frequent in the juvenilia. But now these fantasies have become painfully real for her. She continues, imagining that writing to an old pupil cannot be a very interesting occupation for him, then desperately conceding, "for me it is life itself." Were he to forbid her to write or refuse to reply, that would be to tear from her "the only joy I have on earth." While this language is desperate, it is arguably an exact analysis of her life. Daily life at Haworth had become, for her, joyless. What is unreasonable is any hope that such a serious-minded, hardworking, and morally conventional man could possible change that reality.

Evidently no reply ever arrived. Nine months later she began *Jane Eyre*. The novel can thus be seen as a continuation of her letters to him; the book she had promised if her eyesight did not fail. We can now more fully understand that the novel imagines the passionate love and intense personal involvement Heger denied her as being offered to the heroine Jane Eyre, who so fully resembles Charlotte.

But before Brontë began writing that novel, she had to write another, and it too, in a more obvious way, is about her secret history, and it too is a sad and bewildered effort to reach out to her lost master.

Charlotte Brontë began her first, full-fledged novel during the winter of 1846. At the same time, Emily was working on *Wuthering Heights* and Anne on *Agnes Grey*. Charlotte's first working-title for this book was *The Master*. Read in the light of Charlotte's secret history, *The Professor* takes on particular significance in being, before *Jane Eyre*, Charlotte's most recent exploration of the master motif. In it we find an exploration of the emotional dynamic between a male teacher and an unusual female student. Which is to say, it is all about Charlotte and M. Heger, and it constitutes her first effort to deal with her feelings for him.

Its narrator is an Englishman, William Crimsworth. As we have seen in Chapter Five, in choosing a male narrator, Brontë is following her regular practice during the years when she and Branwell wrote their Angrian saga. Then, Charlotte may have preferred to use the male voice because it seemed to put her on a more equal footing with her brother in their sibling rivalry for dominance. Further, like her preference for using a pseudonym, it deepens her disguise, allowing her to write about her secrets without detection.

Crimsworth takes employment as a teacher of English at a "Pensionnat de demoiselles" on the same Rue d'Isabelle occupied by Mme. Heger's school and is directed by Mdlle. Reuter. Though Crimsworth, just as Charlotte Brontë, is dismayed by the worldliness of the young female students, all of this falls into insignificance as he begins to notice one of his students, the Swiss-English Mdl. Frances Henri: slight, "anxious and preoccupied," with a "careworn" forehead and a mouth that conveys surprise. This is Charlotte Brontë as she must have first appeared to M. Heger. In the novel she gives voice to what she imagines his first reactions to her were. It is also, of course, how Mr. Rochester first views Jane Eyre. In these scenes of emerging love the sequence from fact to fiction is invariable: the sad fact of Charlotte and Heger, followed by the fictional extrapolations of Frances and Crimsworth, Jane Eyre and Mr. Rochester. Except that in the first of the three the love is one-sided and hence thwarted, and, in the end, a source of a frustrated desire and pain that the novels seek to rectify. For Charlotte Brontë, writing became a way for imagination to liberate her from the trammels of painful reality—the "truth" that she aspired both to render and to transcend—and in these fictions Brontë and her readers find a way to something happier and more fulfilling.

Crimsworth soon learns that to earn her lessons, Frances must train other students in needlework, and while "she liked to learn, [she] hated to teach." Insubordinate pupils ignore her pleas for order. A difficulty Frances shares with Charlotte Brontë during her years at Roe Head.

Then, one evening, Crimsworth sits down to read her first essay, what he names "the poor teacher's manuscript," expecting that now he would "see a glimpse of what she really is." Indeed, that is exactly what happens. Almost at once he finds that the essay is unique in its conception and imagination. He admits that he had seen nothing like it in "the course of my professorial experience." When he voices his praise a "transfigured . . . almost triumphant" smile crosses her face, which seems to be asking, "Do you think I am a stranger to myself?" Skipping over M. Heger's tart criticism of her devoirs written under his tutelage, Charlotte imagines this altered version of her "master" immediately recognizes the powers she has known from youth, and her triumph is to find them finally ratified by him. It's a moment of wish-fulfillment for her. A scene she longed for but has never experienced.

We might call this "the test." Charlotte had experienced it during her two years under Heger's tuition, but never with this kind of successful outcome. Soon, as we shall see, Jane Eyre too must face this test. In each instance when the woman's work succeeds, it not only succeeds in winning a just estimate of her work but also of her inner worth, and in so doing it establishes a kinship between the man who judges and the woman he is judging. His admiration validates a specific kind of relationship between them, which Rochester is later to call "a cord of communion." It becomes the basis for Jane Eyre's later defiant claim that she has "as much soul" as he does, and that if her spirit could address his beyond the limits of custom and convention, that they would be "equal—as we are!" Brontë never, up to the publication of *Jane Eyre*, experienced this validation. But in her first two novels she lives vicariously through her heroines who do.

Soon, because of Crimsworth's interest and his praise, Frances undergoes a physical transformation. Her look of wan emaciation, her thoughtful, thin face, blooms with a new "clearness of skin," and "a plumpness almost embonpoint" softened the decided lines of her features. His admiration gives her a new life.

The jealous Mdlle. Reuter, much like the chilly Mme. Heger, faults Frances: "she rather needs keeping down." She is made to echo Southey's letter: "*literary* ambition" is not for "a woman." Rather, she should remain "a respectable, decorous female." This judgment had remained stamped in Charlotte's memory, and now it reappears in the mouth of the hateful and narrow-minded school mistress just as Frances, a character so clearly representative of Charlotte Brontë's wishes and dreams, achieves a highly personal, albeit secret, victory. Charlotte answers Southey and the censorious, self-satisfied women in power from her past life through success in writing that creates a bond between her heroines and the men they desire.

The jealous Reuter expels Frances as an inadequate teacher whose "sphere of life" is beneath that of her pupils. In desperation Frances writes to Crimsworth, and in this amazing and public reiteration of Brontë's experience she writes him, as Brontë had written to Heger, that she is "heart-broken" to be separated from him. But quite unlike Brontë's actual experience, this letter succeeds. William pursues Frances, finding her in a Protestant cemetery. When she realizes he has sought her out, an "animated flush and shining . . . light" appears in her face, and he recognizes in her the "love the courage of a strong heart." Her first words to him are "Mon maître!"—"My master!"

Many elements of the novel's final pages anticipate *Jane Eyre*. Frances Henri accepts William's offer of marriage: "Master, I should be *glad* to live with you always." This time, there is no Mme. Heger, no Bertha Mason to stand in the way. However, again anticipating Jane, Frances refuses to be a financially dependent "incumbrance" on her husband, instead insisting that she will live "an active life," and he agrees—"you shall have your own way." Eventually the husband and wife return to England where they direct a prosperous school. She cares for the children of their institution, anticipating Brontë's later Miss Temple: when a pupil is sick or longs for home, "the Directress spread a wing of kindliest protection," and she summons those who are in need to her "salon to receive some little dole of cake or fruit . . . to be spoken to gently and softly comforted . . . and when bed-time came, dismissed with a kiss of true tenderness." Every element here anticipates the parallel scene in *Jane Eyre*. Certainly this is Charlotte Brontë's imaginative projection of what her life would have become had she won Heger's heart; as a couple they would somehow be exemplars of learning, have sympathy for others, and mutual respect. One of the many problems with *The Professor* is the raw simplicity of it all. When Brontë began *Jane Eyre* she had learned that things are not usually this easy and that the imagination must be disciplined by reference to the bitter facts of ordinary life. Charlotte will meet Heger again, in the dusk, on the road to Hay, but there will be many problems, complications, and losses too before their final reconciliation.

❧

Jane and Rochester achieve their "cord of communion" through a series of tests. Rochester usually engineers them, acting as the master, but Jane Eyre is at the same time testing him. As their mutual love intensifies, he becomes progressively more dependent on her approval. This leads to scenes in which he outright begs for her sympathy and cooperation.

But in their first evening conversation Rochester imagines he is in charge. Jane admits, "it was rather a trial to appear" before him, "formally summoned." After a series of general questions, Rochester begins assessing her abilities, demanding that she demonstrate the kind of ladylike trivial skills taught at a typical school for girls like Lowood. Has she learned some music? There is the piano: "play a tune." Jane puts up with this. Perhaps because she must. Perhaps because she's enjoying his attention. It's the first time in her life anyone like this has treated her this way. She performs. He judges—assuming he's competent to do so—"You play *a little* . . . " This is mockery, an echo of the verbal modesty all young women were expected to adopt in characterizing such a skill. She doesn't demure at this. He's probably right. But now, he's in for something unexpected.

Rochester demands to see her portfolio—sketches, watercolors. Another ladylike skill, which was practiced, as we have seen, by Charlotte Brontë, whose pictorial work was frequently cloying and tedious, typical of what was expected in boarding school. What follows is one of the most remarkable scenes in the novel, woven out of Brontë's vivid past.

As with the earlier exchanges this too is a test, in which Rochester puts himself up as judge assessing Jane's work. That is to say, he steps into the role of M. Heger. In Brussels it was Heger who took up and read Charlotte's assigned essays written in French. He scrutinized them in great detail. As Mr. Rochester glances at Jane's pictures in this scene from 1846–1847, consider a comparison with Heger in Brussels reading and commenting on one of Charlotte's devoirs from April 30, 1842. Unlike many of the topics Heger

assigned, usually historical and religious in nature, this essay seems
to be about something of Charlotte's immediate interest. The twenty-
six-year-old student has written a couple of pages on "The Nest."

Birds are important throughout *Jane Eyre,* from the novel's first
scene in which Jane leafs through Bewick's *British Birds* to the many
later analogies that Rochester draws between its heroine and bird
life. Jane has always been in a very real sense without a home, a nest,
as she has been without a family, and so here the narrator of Charlotte's French essay, in a very similar frame of mind, views with sympathetic delight "a Nest, and in the nest a bird, of what kind I do not
know." Her narrator sees only its head and its eye, large, moist, and
brilliant with which it seemed to follow her every movement. The
narrator looks closer and perceives two eggs, pure as two pearls. She
reaches for them, and the small bird seeks to defend them by making
efforts "to pierce me with its little beak." Heger suggests altering this
to "its resistance, feeble but intrepid, halted my movement and con-
quered my cupidity." The narrator walks on, reflecting on the "courage in the heart of a creature ordinarily so timid and so fearful." In
his comments at the end of the essay, Heger suggests that Charlotte
accentuate everything that sets the main idea in relief, so that the
impression is colorful, picturesque. "It's sufficient," he writes, "that
the rest be <u>in its proper place, but in half-tone</u>. That is what gives to
style, as to painting, unity, perspective, and <u>effect</u>."

The relationship here, as often elsewhere in these school exercises,
is of great importance. Charlotte, formerly a teacher herself, now
receives specific instruction articulated with a sense of authority by a
man she is falling in love with. As we've seen in one of her letters from
Brussels, she actually likes this subservience. The essay's subject,
quickly seen to be analogous to Charlotte, the tiny bird in hiding
with secret treasures that she wishes to defend from the touch of

others, is handed over for Heger's scrutiny and intrusive corrections, permitting him to change what she's done according to his taste. And crucially in this instance it's Heger who, recognizing the strongly visual aspect of Charlotte's imagination, writes in his comments on the similarity between picture and text. The focused and detailed attention Heger gave to Charlotte's essays had to seem to her the kind of attention her writing had never before received. He cares about her. He sees her talent, and she feels grateful for his recognition. Charlotte remembers what this feels like. The electricity of the moment returns as she depicts the scene in the drawing room at Thornfield.

As Rochester sorts through Jane's work, he sweeps away as useless all but three of her pictures. In doing this he chooses the Jane Eyre who interests him. The grilling recommences, perhaps much like the tutorial sessions in Brussels. Where was she when she made these pictures? When? And, most importantly, was she "happy" when she made them? To which Jane gives the most extraordinary response: to paint them "was to enjoy one of the keenest pleasures I have ever known." Rochester tries to brush this aside, assuming there have been but few pleasures at all in Jane's young life. But his observation is simply to feint away from what Jane is telling him, that she is an artist, and in making these pictures she wasn't just "happy," she was more intensely and pleasurably alive than in any other moment in her life. She adds, to the reader, using a term that she will later echo at the moment when she finally tells Rochester she loves him, that she first saw these pictures "with the spiritual eye" before she began to paint them. These moments of autobiographical confession echo and describe Charlotte Brontë's earlier experiences as a writer of the Angrian chronicles and of the very scenes from *Jane Eyre* we are now exploring, written during a convulsive three weeks of unstoppable inspiration.

The dynamic of the moment then is, crucially, this: Rochester instinctively finds the three paintings by Jane that artistically depict the most intense, and private, aspects of who she is. They constitute a visual autobiography, and one that he immediately recognizes as "her," even if he's by no means ready to understand her at all. Still, the intimacy between them has suddenly increased. They are spinning the "cord of communion."

And what amazing pictures they are. While there are traces of the work of some of the painters and engravers Brontë knew—John Martin, for example—and certainly Bewick—these pictures are, if not without precedent, still strikingly odd and unusual for her time, and they anticipate in an uncanny way the work of Symbolist painters such as Odilon Redon, Arnold Böcklin, and Gustav Moreau from the end of the nineteenth century, three to five decades after Brontë imagined them. Her descriptions are long and deserve to be read in their entirety, but here I select just a few salient elements.

In the first we see clouds rolling over "a swollen sea;" no land in sight. Nearby the mast of a half-submerged wrecked ship on which a cormorant, a sea bird proverbial for its gluttonous devouring of fish, is perched. In its beak, a golden bracelet. Sinking into the water, the "fair arm" of a "drowned corpse," "whence the bracelet had been washed or torn."

In the second, against the backdrop of a distant hill and twilight sky, the bust of a woman with dark, wild eyes and streaming hair, and on her "dim forehead," a star.

In the third, distant flickering northern lights. In the foreground "a colossal head" rests against an iceberg. A sable veil, brow bloodless as bone, an eye hollow and fixed with despair. Above the head a fiery white ring.

While Jane names the second the "Evening Star," and the third

"The likeness of a Kingly Crown," these labels are altogether inadequate to convey the mysterious richness of the pictures described and the woman who made them. Rochester offers what is clearly an uncomprehending response, teasing Jane that they are "elfish," and that they must have been—and here he is a bit closer to the mark—"seen in a dream." To his question as to whether it took a long time to execute them Jane replies, "I sat at them from morning till noon, and from noon till night . . . " Charlotte seems to recall one of her own experiences when she spent a great part of almost every day of a vacation visit to Bolton Abbey in drawing or painting, working, as Ellen Nussy later recalled, "for nine hours with scarcely an interval."

The obsessive dedication to the making of these images tells us that—for Jane who painted them and also for Charlotte who evokes them in prose—they are revelatory. All three depict allegorical female figures, and the first and third take us back to Bewick's northern scenes of stormy seas, shipwrecks, icebergs, and isolated birds, a world the reclusive Jane and Charlotte instinctively felt to be theirs. Death's horror dominates the first and third, while the second, moonlit scene, seems to depict a vatic, visionary woman whose eyes see something "dark and wild." Nightmarish, yes, these are symbolic visions that invite virtually endless speculation, yet clearly indicate at least one thing: Jane Eyre and, certainly in this instance, her creator Charlotte Brontë see with a "spiritual eye" into frightful realms. They recapitulate and extend the novel's initial discussion of Bewick rendering Jane Eyre's inner life, her solitude, fears, vision of a death-filled and meaningless world.

Certainly Rochester realizes even at this early moment that in Jane he is not dealing with just any governess. Discoveries such as this are the basis for the love story to follow. From the start it is of the spirit. Rochester has had more than his fill of blowsy superficial beauty that he has already swept aside. And, crucially, he likes, admires, and is becoming involved in "the shadow of your thought," which he discerns in the pictures and in the sensibility of the enigmatic woman who expressed it. Heger's comments on Charlotte's "The Nest" essay are, typically for him, cool, cautious, professional. He offers advice on writing technique. Rochester's remarks express a personal curiosity for and admiration of the spirit of the woman who has created them, something Heger may have been careful not to voice but Charlotte surely longed for.

The house party scenes are Rochester's next test. He tortures Jane through exposure and envy in an effort to strengthen the cord of communion that they both are starting to feel. And he succeeds. Wearily Jane concedes: "He made me love him without looking at me." Her pain is closely akin to the torment which Charlotte Brontë describes in her desperate letters to M. Heger. But because Jane recognizes that this comes from a Mr. Rochester who wishes to test and manipulate her, the experience is paradoxically consoling and promising. Heger's silence and distance become transformed into Mr. Rochester's obtrusive scene setting and performing. He's doing this all for her.

While at first glance these chapters might seem remote from Charlotte Brontë's past experiences, they are in fact woven together from much that she had seen and done—some of it recounted in Chapter Four in its discussion of Charlotte Brontë's adolescent years—coupled ingeniously with elaborate fantasy imaginings about wealth, status, elegance, and decadence prominent in her youthful writing about "high society" in the world of Angria. Hence a great deal of what goes on in these scenes is just as autobiographical as the rest of *Jane Eyre.*

Hiding in the "sanctum" or "refuge" of the schoolroom, Jane observes the guests arriving just as Charlotte, when a young governess at Stonegappe, found that house noisy with visits from friends and family members of her employers who "bewildered the shy governess" as she watched their arrival from her second-story room. Rochester knows their appearance will alarm Jane. Charlotte too had felt this way about encountering new people since her early visits to the Nussey family back in 1832. In trying to account for this, Ellen was later to remember that the young Charlotte was so painfully shy that one day on being led to dinner by a stranger she was trembling and near tears. Nussey had a wise explanation for this: Charlotte's shyness was the consequence of her "<u>not</u> being understood." She felt apart from others. This is exactly Jane Eyre's subsequent reaction. Observing Rochester's guests she says, "I had no sympathy with their appearance, their expression." The reader of *Jane Eyre* knows its heroine/narrator quite well by this time. The alienation she feels at the arrival of these socialites is something the reader shares with her. There is no way, even if these people did wish to get to know her—which, as it turns out, they do not—that they could. Like Charlotte, she is too different from them. Charlotte understood this keenly when with the Sidgewicks on their summer holiday in June of 1839; she felt "the miseries of a reserved wretch like me." She found herself thrown at once into the midst of "a large Family—proud as peacocks and wealthy as Jews," at a time when they were particularly gay, the house was filled with company, and all of them "[s]trangers people whose faces I had never seen before." She soon came to realize that a private governess "has no existence" for these people and "is not considered as a living and rational" person, except for the duties she was expected to fulfill.

Rochester, knowing Jane's antipathies, now forces her to join the guests in the drawing room where a large fire burns silently on the marble hearth, and wax candles shine amid exquisite flowers. The young Charlotte had gleefully imagined such a place in her 1834 *High Life in Verdopolis* where she had pictured a

> vista of proud saloons, glowing with brilliant fires & dazzling chandeliers, whose warm ruddy beams slept on rich carpets, silken sofas, cushions, ottomans, Gleaming groups of statuary, sideboard where the flash of plate & glass almost blinded the eye that gazed on them, ample tables covered with splendid engravings, portfolios, magnificently bound volumes, Gold musical boxes, enameled Miniature vases, Guitars of elaborate & beautiful workmanship, clocks & lamps of alabaster & ormolu, &c., &c., &c.

Much of this litter of expensive and useless things is to reappear during the ensuing pages of *Jane Eyre*. Such ostentatious wealth delighted Charlotte Brontë as the youthful author of *High Life*, but now she is quite a different woman. After her visits with Amelia Walker and months with the Sidgwick family, Brontë has come to assess the worthlessness of these objects and the way they function in the upside-down value system of the wealthy. She writes here autobiographically, from personal experience, and on this bases her judgments.

Jane, from the corner of the drawing room, observes the ladies, dominated by the Dowager Lady Ingram. We already know her well. Her "fierce and hard eye," Jane tells us, "reminded me of Mrs.

Reed." She is but the latest in Charlotte's gallery of dominating older women, "very pompous, very dogmatical—very intolerable, in short." She is Mrs. Sidgwick, and particularly Mme. Heger; rivals who instinctively distrusted Charlotte just as Mrs. Reed distrusted Jane because they are different in body, conduct, and spirit. Rochester forced her to attend to antagonize Jane and to introduce her daughter Blanche, Jane's antitype. Blanche Ingram is much like her mother, "the same low brow, the same high features, the same pride." Tall, robust, "dark as a Spaniard," and, though Jane cannot know this at the time, remarkably like Rochester's wife. These women are to interpose themselves in one way or another between Jane and the man she recklessly is coming to love.

Brontë had been exploring for years the opposition between these two female types. In her *Henry Hastings* of 1838 she opposes the triumphant Jane Moore to the Elizabeth Hastings we have already met, the "pale, under-sized young woman," who dresses as plainly as a Quakeress in gray. Charlotte pictures Jane Moore as quite the opposite of the later Jane Eyre, a young woman who "shone in blond and satin." She displays her neck and arms knowing plainly enough that both were as white and round and statuesque "as if Phidias had got up from the dead to chisel them out of the purest marble." Trappings of wealth set her off: pearls circling her neck and arms indicate that she had taste enough to be aware how effective was the contrast between the dazzling, living flesh and the cold, glistening gem. "She was a superb animal." In contrast to Jane Moore's ostentatious performance, Elizabeth's features were masked. Her "movements were restrained and guarded." Her reserve and caution anticipate Jane Eyre's. Blanche Ingram is, like Jane Moore, "remarkably self-conscious." She flaunts herself before the other guests, bent on striking them as "dashing and daring." Seating herself at the piano she announces she will sing a "Corsair-song. Know that I doat on Corsairs; and for that reason, sing it 'con spirito." She looks and sounds ridiculous. It's Byron's poem *The Corsair* of 1814 to which the song alludes. Its protagonist Conrad is, like Byron's Giaour, one of Charlotte Brontë's sources for Mr. Rochester: "his dark eyebrow shades a glance of fire . . . Sun-burnt his cheek, his forehead high and pale . . . " Soon enough Blanche realizes that her cumbersome and foolish rhetoric will fail to overcome the attractive power of silent Jane. She will overthrow this fine lady through a kind of integrity Blanche cannot even understand.

Taking Jane aside toward the end of the evening, Rochester asks if she is "a little depressed"? Would a few more words "bring tears to your eyes . . . "? This calculated cruelty, and his relishing of Jane Eyre's unhappiness, stems directly from Charlotte's Zamorna. Here is just one example from *High Life in Verdopolis*. By now the irony of that title is quite clear. In one scene Zamorna tortures his faithful and loving wife Mary Percy. They're in the middle of a lavish party. Zamorna expels a guest who has been spending too much time with Mary and then turns to look at his wife with a "cold & haughty smile," while the gloom that comes across his forehead suggests something far different. Mary, turning "white as death & sick with agitation" collapses in a nearby chair. "Are you better?" he asks coldly. Tears swell in her eyes, and she looks reproachfully at the "disdainful & jealous Despot." Taking the hand of a nearby young and beautiful woman, Zamorna turns his back on Mary and leads the other woman onto the dance floor. Mary remains in an alcove burdened with "the heaviness of a sorrowful heart." Seeing her melancholy from a distance, Zamorna returns to his wife for a fond and intimate conversation as he confesses, "I am infernally jealous." And then abruptly orders her, "Leave your husband . . . to find his own faults if he has done wrong, & never either by inference or direct assertion show him where they lie." Charlotte as the young author of such scenes seems to have found Zamorna's ruthless dominance exciting. But by the time she writes *Jane Eyre*, she is far more fully aware of how cruel her heroes can be. At the same time, in the scenes with Blanche we see emerging a quiet victory not only over her but also over Rochester. Yes, he wants to hurt Jane into love. But it is he who keeps finding moments to leave the crowd and, like Zamorna, solicitously ask how she is reacting. It's her silent endurance that is winning him. The little governess is made of sterner stuff.

Blanche doesn't stand a chance against Jane, but there is another woman with a strange, pervasive presence at Thornfield Hall. During Jane's first day, as Mrs. Fairfax shows her the third story, she hears her curious laugh—"distinct, formal, mirthless." This woman will constitute the climactic trial or test for Jane Eyre's time at Thornfield. It's now time to get to know her better and to inquire how much Charlotte Brontë knew about her. And why Charlotte might consider that knowledge something she prefers to keep secret.

8

The Fury

The mysterious female figure who haunts Thornfield Hall comes from the traditions of gothic fiction. There is no direct evidence that Charlotte Brontë ever read the classic gothic novels of the eighteenth and early nineteenth centuries such as Horace Walpole's *The Castle of Otranto*, Matthew Gregory Lewis' *The Monk*, or the novels of Ann Radcliffe. Instead, she makes clear in a letter to Hartley Coleridge that she reveled in writing from this tradition that she found in "ladies magazines," often reading them in secret "with the most exquisite pleasure," and she playfully suggests that had she been older she might have written stories with fanciful titles such as "Count Albert or the haunted castle— Evelina or the Recluse of the Lake—Sigismund or the Nunnery." One recurrent characteristic of many texts from this tradition is that the specters and monsters that terrify are in the end fully explained in rational and materialistic terms. So in *Jane Eyre* the reader eventually learns that what haunts Thornfield Hall is a real woman, and in meticulous detail Brontë accounts for her presence, her physical characteristics, and her motives. The Creole daughter of a rich Anglo-Jamaican family, Bertha Mason attracts the young Fairfax Rochester when he is sent to the Caribbean to make his fortune. After their marriage she quickly degenerates into loathsome bestiality. Unable to tolerate life with her, Rochester takes her back to the family estate in England and locks his wife, now a raving madwoman, into the third-floor attic prison, from which she sometimes escapes to seek revenge.

As with so much in this novel, what appears to be fantastic and improbable emerges from Charlotte Brontë's past experiences as a writer and a woman. Bertha Mason turns out, as we will now see, to have striking kinship affinities to the woman who invents her.

For one thing, Bertha is a figure who from early on haunted Brontë's imagination. Brontë's juvenilia offer striking parallels. A figure like Bertha already dominates one of her earliest stories, "The Fairy Gift," written when she was fourteen. The first-person narrator, an unremarkable, ordinary guy, tells a kind of fairy tale that begins with a diminutive man in green who appears with a magic ring which will grant his wishes. The narrator asks for beauty and the next morning he has become tall, slender, and graceful, with a peculiarly feminine loveliness. His transformed complexion is now of the "purest red and white;" his eyes swim in "liquid radiance" under the narrow dark arches of two exquisitely formed eyebrows; his mouth is of a "winning sweetness."

His new beauty attracts the attention of Lady Ducie, already middle-aged, who is wealthy, "fat and ugly" with "the reputation of being a witch." Visiting her castle the narrator notes her "stout, lusty figure" and "her brawny shoulders." Ducie anticipates the family wealth and over-size attractions of Bertha Mason, just as the narrator's prettiness suggests the youthful and naïve Fairfax Rochester. She offers marriage, and, given her wealth and power, the narrator accepts. They wed three weeks later.

He moves into her mansion marveling at its "vast halls and magnificent apartments." But, much like the young Rochester, he soon grows unhappy. He becomes, in his ignorance, "lost in my own house," a place with many passages and galleries he had never seen before. Alienated, like Rochester living in Spanish Town, he finds his wife's "high-bred guests" despise him for his clownish manners. The servants insult him.

As time passes a transformation takes place, similar to what was to happen to Bertha. Just as Bertha's rage emerges, Lady Ducie's temper shows itself every day more and more in the most "hideous light." She becomes terribly jealous and will hardly permit him to leave her sight for a moment. The narrator's flirtation with another woman, Cecilia Standon, prompts Lady Ducie to threaten revenge. That night, like Jane Eyre, he hears footsteps outside his chamber door. Through the darkness he follows Lady Ducie who is carrying a lighted candle in her hand, just as Bertha is later to prowl the second-floor corridor at Thornfield. She goes to the gothic tradition's classic damp, subterraneous vault. Flames dart out of the earth, circling her "like fiery snakes," and huge smoldering clouds of smoke roll over the slimy walls. Six "black, indefinable figures" appear bearing the corpse of poor Cecilia. The narrator screams in horror and Lady Ducie, enraged, seizes him by the throat and attempts to strangle him—just as Bertha attacks Rochester. However, as events reach a crisis, suddenly she crumples and dies. The fairy man in green wielding a bloody knife is seen. He has stabbed her "through the heart."

This extravagant early story, emerging from Charlotte's youthful and unbridled imagination, significantly anticipates Brontë themes that Bertha Mason is to repeat—melodramatic differences between the rich and poor, the danger in being drawn into the control of the powerful, the mysterious palace, the physically dominant older woman, her lascivious degeneration, entrapment, violent attack.

From the early tale to the adult novel, Brontë remains persistently interested in size. It's her own, diminutive physical presence that makes her so aware of the bodies of others. The female enemies of her fictions are big women: Lady Ducie, stout, lusty, and brawny; Mrs. Reed, dark skinned, square shouldered, her "under jaw" prominent; the Dowager Lady Ingram, tall, of an "imperial dignity," with a throat like a "pillar"; and her daughter Blanche, in her physical imperiousness much like her mother. Bertha is yet another of these. Charlotte wishes recurrently to stress the similarities. Blanche's deceptive name doesn't mask the fact that she is "dark as a Spaniard." Rochester mockingly describes her as "a real strapper . . . big, brown and buxom," with black hair just like the "ladies of Carthage." When he finally reveals the truth about Bertha, he immediately notes that when he first met her, she was exactly "in the style of" Blanche, tall, dark, imposing. When Jane first watches him struggling to subdue her, she sees a woman who is "big" with "virile force." In a binary, these women are all the "not-Jane."

Charlotte Brontë was, by dramatic contrast, a tiny woman. Just like Jane Eyre. Very short, with, as Gaskell, who knew her well as an adult, tells us, a "slight, fragile" body, her hands and feet the "smallest I ever saw," the touch of her hand like "the soft touch of a bird in the middle of my palm." Her antagonists, the not-Jane, stem from the belligerent women of her past life: Miss Miller the abusive teacher at Cowan Bridge, Mrs. Sidgwick her imperious and dismissive employer at Stonegappe, and later Mme. Heger, represented in *The Professor* by Mdlle. Reuter. Some of these women were not the physically imposing foes of Brontë's fiction, but Charlotte's antagonism embodies in them their domineering natures. *The Professor's* narrator Crimsworth depicts Reuter/Heger as a woman searching for the weak points in his character, applying now this test, now that, hoping in the end to find some chink, some niche where she could put in her firm foot and "stand up on my neck." Violence is typical of these women. It articulates their inherent cruelty. Showing Bertha to the priest and the lawyer on the day of his aborted wedding with Jane, Rochester asks the two of them to compare the opposites of the binary: "this form with that bulk." He speaks for Charlotte, who wishes the world to compare her tiny self with her adversaries.

In creating Bertha, Brontë's imagination works with what she considered to be the material realities of the early nineteenth century— the world that she had read about in books and magazines, and which she had already drawn into her earlier fictions.

The Glasstown/Angrian fantasy writings are about the imperialist adventure—Europeans taking over and colonizing an invented South Africa, transforming it into a new and economically powerful country. Rochester's life story recapitulates this narrative. The second son of an "avaricious" father, he is to inherit nothing and so is coerced to travel to Jamaica, the Caribbean English colony where since 1655 large fortunes had been made through the production of sugarcane on plantations farmed by slaves from Africa. By the early nineteenth century, the ratio of black to white in the island population was twenty to one. Brontë knows this, and her novel seems indifferent to the profound injustice of the colonial system. It is, however, fascinated by racial difference.

In Rochester's telling of his experiences, what matters about them is ethnicity. And in this the not-Jane gets a particular formulation. He heads to Jamaica anticipating an arranged marriage with the daughter of a wealthy merchant and planter named Mason, whose possessions were "real and vast." Mason wants the wedding because, crucially, Rochester is of "a good race." In Bertha he finds a young woman who lavishly displays her "charms" and is bewildered and "stimulated" by her. There is a strong erotic attraction in her dark looks. He never meets her mother and is misled into thinking she is dead. This is a ruse. The reason is that the woman is Creole, that is, of mixed race, and had degenerated into a drunkard and a madwoman. Herein Brontë's use of difference becomes quite sinister. After marriage Bertha quickly changes: Rochester soon learns what a "pigmy" intellect she has—the adjective reflecting her African origins—what "giant propensities"—naming her animal absence of self-control. According to Brontë's worldview, hereditary racial degeneration will out. With her mother in a lunatic asylum and one brother "a complete dumb idiot," Bertha begins to indulge her vices, becoming "intemperate and unchaste." The other brother, who comes to England to reveal the truth about his concealed and imprisoned sister, is soon to degenerate into madness as well.

This lurid portrayal of ethnically inherited degeneration as Brontë imagined it—derived from African descent—had appeared early in the fantasy writings of her youth, centrally in a character she and Branwell named Quashia, of the indigenous Ashantee tribe. Uncontrollably passionate, lascivious, and treacherous, he recurrently appears in the Glasstown and later Angrian tales as the foe of the European colonizers. Brontë loved to entertain him in her fantasies. While trapped into teaching at Roe Head, for example, her journal there records one evening in which, escaping from her duties, she begins, in a dreamy reverie, to picture an idealized young and very European lady with a book in her hand, her head bent gently over it as she reads. This morphed version of herself, not poor, plain, and repressed but rather rich, attractive, at leisure, suddenly finds her "hallowed and shrine-like separation" violated by Quashia, seemingly attractive in his very animality: his sable hair disheveled on his forehead, his "tusk-like teeth" glancing vindictively through his parted lips, his brown complexion flushed with wine, his broad chest "heaving wildly," his breath issuing in "snorts" from his "distended nostrils."

Brontë's Englishness also found morally degenerate alien others in her only experience of a foreign country, Belgium. She came to detest her pupils in Brussels: she wrote to Branwell that they lacked "intellect" and "politeness or good-nature or good-feeling—they are nothing." This, she was convinced, was the consequence of their ethnicity. She considered the Belgians without passion. The "phlegm that thickens their blood is too gluey to boil." Blood is again the issue. Hence her time there in 1843 was intensely lonely. She had the same feelings for her fellow instructors such as Mme. Blanche whom she described as false and contemptible. "She perceives my utter dislike and never now speaks to me." Brontë spurns the other.

Worse still, from her perspective, is a female character, also linked to the tropics, who appears in *The Professor* as one of William Crimsworth's students. Juanna Trista, of Belgian and Spanish origin, is born on an unnamed Caribbean island and comes to Brussels for her education. Pale-complected with dark hair and eyes, she has a "gaunt visage" and looked "fierce and hungry." In class she makes noises with her mouth "like a horse" and "ejected saliva" as she "uttered brutal expressions." Antagonistic to Crimsworth from the start, Juanna gathers a crowd of like-minded girls making a "swinish tumult." She remains in Europe only long enough to repay by "malevolence and ingratitude" all who have ever done her a good turn. Then she returns to the Isles, exulting in the thought that she should there have slaves whom, as she said, she could "kick and strike at will." Naturally she is the opposite of the pale, Frances Henri, the character so like Charlotte Brontë, with whom Crimsworth is soon to fall in love.

Rochester's bitter narrative of his relationship to the French opera-dancer Céline Varens becomes a further instance of Brontë's persistent depiction of ethnic/racial difference. Her very smell, of "musk and amber," is anything but "the odor of sanctity," and soon he overhears her with another lover, a *vicomte*. Their conversation is "frivolous, mercenary, heartless, and senseless." Hence, from Brontë's perspective, as French as their decadent moral conduct, the "slime and mud of Paris."

Rochester condemns himself, in his conversations with Jane Eyre, for the naïve ignorance that seduced him into these previous relationships. He strives to exert English, masculine control over Céline's daughter Adèle through Jane Eyre. She succeeds as a governess, as Charlotte Brontë had not in real life, in domesticating the little girl. Bertha Mason proves far more intractable—hence the third-floor prison.

This was nothing new to Charlotte Brontë. From time to time she had heard about and even witnessed the practical questions of dealing with the insane. There were places she had visited: the attic rooms at Norton Conyers with their legend of an imprisoned madwoman, and, more importantly, the padded cell at North Lees Hall. Brontë visited this country house in 1845, a year before she began

Jane Eyre. This ancient, battlemented hall was then inhabited by the widowed Mary Eyre, her son George, and three daughters. There Charlotte saw the Eyre monument in the local parish church and also the apostle cupboard, which makes a dramatic appearance in Chapter XX of *Jane Eyre,* on the night when Bertha Mason attacks her brother leaving him soaked in blood. The first mistress of North Lees, Agnes Ashurst, "reputedly went mad, was confined in a padded rom, and died in a fire." Here Brontë may well have found the name of her heroine, some crucial elements of the country estate of Mr. Rochester, and the ultimate fate of the madwoman in its attic. Charlotte also frequently discussed with her close friend Ellen Nussey the plight of her older brother George, who was already seeking treatment for his mental health in 1843. He eventually became an inmate at a private institution in York where he remained until his death in 1885. In all the instances just considered, the troubled, mad, and sometimes even demonic woman or man is seen as "the other," someone radically different from ordinary people. How consoling for Jane, and indeed for Charlotte, is the thought that they don't come from the hot, bestial south, that they are small, reserved, thoughtfully cautious, and rational. Or are they?

❧

"What a fury to fly at Master John!" exclaims Mrs. Reed's servant Abbot as she and Bessie drag Jane Eyre off to the red-room. As Jane mops the blood from the bite wounds of Richard Mason she wonders what "creature" could have done this. "Why had the Fury flown at him?" The Greek mythological furies to whom they both allude— to whom Brontë alludes—are female goddesses described, variously, as having snakes for hair, dog's heads, coal-black bodies, bat's wings, and bloodshot eyes. Their function is to avenge injustice. The most celebrated representation of them is in the *Oresteia* trilogy, plays by Aeschylus first performed in Athens in 485 BC, which describe how the queen Clytemnestra murders her husband Agamemnon and then is in turn murdered by her son Orestes in revenge. The crime, the killing of his mother, draws out from the underworld the furies who merciless pursue him. The uncontrolled anger of these demons reappears, according to the horrified servants at Gateshead, and later in the unspoken thoughts of Jane Eyre at Thornfield, as they witness women transformed by rage. Furies. Jane tells us that during her first day at Thornfield as Mrs. Fairfax shows her the third floor, she hears a "tragic" and "preternatural" laugh that "thrilled me." What is the content, what are the implications of that "thrill"?

In his famous 1919 essay on the "uncanny," Freud describes the experience of this kind of sudden, unexpected, unnerving, indeed "frightening" response—that something is "uncanny"—as "that class of the terrifying which leads us back to something long known to us, once very familiar," but now "concealed and kept out of sight." The experience is of something that is neither new nor foreign but rather of "something familiar and old-established" in the mind that has been estranged from it by the process of repression. And so the uncanny is something that ought to have been kept concealed but which has nevertheless come to light. What thrills Jane in the pre-ternatural laugh? Is there a kinship between twin furies Bertha and Jane? Does Bertha function in Brontë's novel as the grotesque embodiment of that which Jane—and Charlotte who has made Jane in her image and likeness—knows lurks within herself, something fearful and shameful that she has tried to repress? Are there ways in which the murderous rage of Lady Ducie, the cruelty of Juanna, the savagery of Bertha express something suppressed in Brontë's heroine and within Brontë herself? If we are looking for an autobiographical source for the grotesque figure of Bertha Mason, we must look deep within Charlotte herself, at one of her darkest secrets now brought to light. That is what stands behind the locked third-floor door.

⟋⟋⟍

Twice Jane Eyre tries to see herself in a mirror. First, in the red-room. As her rage cools, she discerns in a great looking-glass, which shows a "visionary hollow," a "strange little figure gazing at me." She is "other" to herself. Years later, on the morning of her intended wedding, having seen the face of Bertha hanging over her two nights earlier, "her lurid visage" flaming "over mine," Jane again sees herself in a mirror, seeming "almost the image of a stranger." The first revelation precedes Jane's terror at what she thinks is the apparition of her dead uncle, which throws her into "a species of fit." The second follows the night when for the second and only other time Jane loses consciousness: observing in Bertha a horrific twin gazing down at her, she becomes "insensible from terror." Brontë draws the reader's attention to the interconnections. They lead us into this strange kinship.

While Jane is physically small, there are moments when, overcome with rage, she becomes possessed by an emotional and, indeed, spiritual power that stuns and alarms her formidable foes, forcing them to retreat and capitulate. Weeks after the red-room experience, when Mrs. Reed declares her children should no longer "'associate" with Jane, she shouts from the stairwell: "They are not fit to associate with me." She astonishes herself; what she says seems to her as if her tongue "pronounced words without my will consenting" to the utterance: "something spoke out of me over which I had no control." This something alarms Mrs. Reed, who stares at her as if she cannot be sure whether Jane is a child or a "fiend." Through Jane, Brontë shows how this uncontrolled and unconscious ireful response—her very name points to this aspect of her nature—has a kind of fearful power. Her other self has momentarily taken over in response to the injustice done to her. When subsequently Mrs. Reed insults Jane in front of Brocklehurst, declaring the child is a liar, Jane again begins to experience "ungovernable excitement." She trembles violently, feeling as if "an invisible bond had burst" and in "a savage, high voice" denies the accusation. Years later a dying Mrs. Reed still remembered this confrontation: "she talked to me once like something mad, or like a fiend." She seemed like "an animal . . . with human eyes." Here we are very close to Bertha Mason's rage indeed. A fiend, a savage, an animal—all of these descriptors are echoed when Jane finally comes face to face with Bertha in her prison room. Jane's—and Brontë's—language utterly dehumanizes Bertha. "It snatched and growled like some wild animal." Bertha tries to strangle Rochester and bites his cheek. "At last he mastered her," Jane tells us, relieved as Bertha is tied down in a chair. Exactly as Bessie threatened Jane—"you must be tied down"—when she is dragged to the red-room—Rochester ties down Bertha. The fury, the alien outsider, must be mastered.

At every turn, Jane Eyre's narrative leads us to accept the interpretation that she is a victim, that her moments of unconscious rage liberate a power deep within her which cries out for justice. Bertha is not offered the same sympathy in the text. But Charlotte Brontë does at least offer the novel's reader information that permits an alternative interpretation of what has happened to Bertha Mason—from her point of view. If Jane finds being locked into the red-room terrifying and infuriating, so too would a native of Jamaica accustomed to a life of luxury, admiring male attention, heavy drinking, and sexual adventure find her locked third-floor room and gloomy servant Grace Poole anything but pleasant. In the rare moments when Bertha is able to escape, she emerges as a vengeful spirit from Rochester's past, a version of the ghost of Uncle Reed or of the specter Elinor from Brontë's poem "Gilbert." Silent, feeling her way through unfamiliar territory, armed only with a candle, she is determined to attack the man who has taken her life from her. Brontë deliberately creates the uncanny coincidences. Bertha tries to burn her husband to death in his bed hours after he confesses his sexual excesses to the virginal intruder Jane Eyre. When Bertha's cringing and feckless brother suddenly appears in her rooms, she seems overcome by a Jane-like rage at his indifference to her unjustifiable imprisonment and his inability to do anything about it. Living on what seems to be a diet of sago gruel, cared for haphazardly by the alcoholic Grace Poole, never permitted to see the light of day or to breathe fresh air, it's no wonder Bertha releases the same frenzied rage Jane experiences. But the kinship goes further.

Consider this confessional moment from one of Charlotte's letters written in 1836 to Ellen Nussey, in which she describes herself as a "coarse common-place wretch!" Brontë insists she has feelings which Ellen "can have no participation in" and that "very few people in the world can at all understand." She confesses that while she strives to suppress them, these feelings sometimes "burst out" and then "those who see the explosion despise me and I hate myself for days afterwards."

Or this remark from December 1846 when she was in the middle of writing *Jane Eyre*:

I daresay I should spit fire and explode sometimes . . . my humor I think is too soon overthrown—too sore—too demonstrative and vehement . . .

Or this, written to Branwell in 1843, when Charlotte was in Brussels, describing her reaction to stupid students—she sometimes would get red-faced but "if I spoke warmly, as warmly as I sometimes used to do at Roe-Head they would think me mad . . ."

There is an important pattern here. Charlotte Brontë acknowledges that her "humor"—which in traditional medical terminology as Charlotte understood it means a physically internal tendency or condition that she has not chosen but must live with—is an inclination to excessive wrath that sometimes bursts from her—uncontrolled, destructive, and hence fearsome. This makes her different from other people and only a very few "in all the world" can understand it. She does what she can to conceal these rages with what Freud calls repression. It's clear they are dramatically different from the self-control and discipline expected of a young clergyman's daughter. They make her despicable to others and herself. They are something to conceal, to hide away and lock up inside of her. In something like a psychological attic prison. She fears that naïve observers such as her stupid pupils witnessing such red-faced passion would think her insane.

The uncanny thrill that Jane experiences when she first hears Bertha laugh, which mounts in terror and intensity as the madwoman gets ever closer to her, comes from their uncanny similarity, a kinship both secretly share with Charlotte Brontë who is imagining them.

Rage structures the way Charlotte Brontë remembers key moments in her life, and it also structures the way she tells Jane Eyre's life story.

Now we can look back at just a few instances.

First, anger and cruelty directed at her inspires consequences for her antagonists. At Cowan Bridge School the clergyman William Carus Wilson threatens the diminutive and fearful eight-year-old with sudden death and eternal damnation. She watches her sickly older sister bullied, manhandled, and shamed by her teachers. Charlotte typically responds with counterattacks. She voices rebellion and distain for Wilson depicting him as Brocklehurst, and for her teachers embodied in the "little and dark personage" Miss Scatcherd. As a teacher in Miss Wooler's school, she describes her pupils as fat heads and dolts, picturing herself "in this wretched bondage, forcibly suppressing my rage at [their] idleness the apathy and the hyperbolical & most asinine stupidity." Later, trying to help support her family, Charlotte as governess must endure Mrs. Sidgwick's "black looks," her zest for "scolding me," using "a sternness of manner & harshness of language scarcely credible. " Her son throws stones at Charlotte. Mrs. White also gives way "to anger in a very coarse unladylike manner . . . [that] is highly offensive." A desperate and lonely Charlotte Brontë finds Mme. Heger coldly ignoring her during summer holidays in Brussels and seeking to bar her from her husband's affections. Back at Haworth she finds that he distances himself from the desperate emotion of her letters, refusing to reply.

Her reaction to many of the young men she encounters is disdainful rejection. Amelia Walker's brother is a "<u>Booby</u>." As for young clergymen, traditionally the most expectable possible future husbands for the oldest daughter of a priest: most "curates . . . seem to me a self-seeking vain, empty race." When three appear for tea at

Haworth one day "they began glorifying themselves and abusing Dissenters," and "my temper lost its balance and I pronounced a few sentences sharply & rapidly which struck them all dumb." The unexpected, unprovoked attack astonishes them. Very like Mrs. Reed's reactions to Jane's similar outbursts.

This sketch of a very few selected instances is in no way intended to argue that Charlotte Brontë was a constantly irritable and angry person. She was merry and loving to her family members and deeply valued by her chosen friends over the course of many years. What it does suggest, however, is that like many people she could get very angry, that these moments of rage troubled her in retrospect, and she tended to conceal them as a dangerous propensity. When it came to inventing Jane Eyre—and Bertha Mason—her preoccupation with and fear of this rage were clearly influences, and she found it important to present and explore that propensity. Charlotte denied, of course, that her heroine was in any way based on her. A denial that is part of the mechanics of the uncanny as Freud describes them.

Bertha's silent intrusion into Jane's bedroom two nights before the scheduled wedding, her tearing of the bridal veil, her close scrutiny of the terrified Jane Eyre, is indeed the Jamaican Creole's assertion of her grim right to the Rochester who has imprisoned her. It is also—and here the uncanny nature of Bertha's kinship with Jane comes most dramatically into view—a warning of what Jane instinctively knows is just about to happen, and what must happen. During the weeks before the wedding, Jane becomes progressively more apprehensive about marriage to a Rochester who seems not only recklessly willful but ever more unaware of Jane's doubts and apprehensions. His jokes about seraglios and harem beauties have made her anxious about what married life is going to be like, and her passive acceptance of most of Rochester's demands, along with her sense that her feelings for him have exceeded sensible limits, turning him from a fallible man into a substitute for God, lead her to speculating that the whole affair has become unreal. On the day of the marriage, Jane's mirror shows her a "stranger." Bertha's tearing of the veil has become an unconscious act of sisterhood. Even before she learns that Rochester's first wife still lives, Jane is alarmed at his frenzied energy and his willful ignorance of her feelings. The morning of the wedding his hand holds her "by a grasp of iron" as he hurries her along at a pace "I could hardly follow." Instinctively, Jane knows the wedding should not take place. It's wrong.

And it doesn't. The moon, Brontë's recurrent figure since Jane's childhood at Lowood school for the mother as guardian figure, echoing Brontë's yearning for her lost mother, appears to Jane in a dream, morphing into "a white human form" gazing down on her from an azure sky, whispering in her heart, "My daughter, flee temptation!"

And she does.

9

Desolation

Jane Eyre is a linear novel narrating a series of efforts by its heroine to escape. Ironically when Jane Eyre struggles to flee Thornfield her seemingly random journey—her only goal is to find somewhere Mr. Rochester has "no connections"—leads Jane to a place very nearly resembling the childhood home of Charlotte Brontë; the place Brontë longed to escape as she wrote this section. To get to that place, to cross a threshold into a new kind of security and happiness, Jane must first struggle through the most dangerous part of her road of trials.

Jane's series of escapes—from Gateshead, Lowood, and now Thornfield—mirror, in an intensely allusive, autobiographical way, Charlotte Brontë's life and her frustrated efforts to break free from its limits. Angrily unhappy as a schoolteacher and governess, for years she hoped her writing would free her to enter the larger world she read about, glimpsed during her journeys to and from Brussels, but never really entered.

The desperation Brontë faced in 1846, as she began writing *Jane Eyre,* is that of a divided self. Jane arises as a fictional manifestation of Charlotte's lived desperation. Leaving Rochester after the terrible revelation of Bertha Mason, Jane finds that she, who had just been "an ardent, expectant woman," has suddenly become "a cold, solitary girl again." All now seems to regress: her life seems pale; her prospects "desolate." The chance for a new life appears permanently denied to her. Matters were exactly the same for Brontë. She found herself thrust back from warm adulthood to a kind of frozen childhood, both cut off from the former delightful escape route of writing the Angrian chronicles with her brother and forced to leave Heger, the man she desired and could not have. Both women are thwarted, denied what they want.

As early as 1815, Patrick Brontë had warned in his prefatory note to his long story *The Cottage in the Wood,* "The mind is its own place. Put a good man any where and he will not be miserable—put a bad man any where and he cannot be happy." With crisp certitude Charlotte's father argues his case. The reason, to him, is obvious: the bad man "carries his mind with him," and this becomes the source of "unruly desires, vain expectation, heavy disappointment, and keen remorse." Her father's counsel bore down heavily on Charlotte in the months after she left Brussels for good.

When Jane flees Thornfield she achieves something Charlotte Brontë could not. And she knew it. During the months when she was writing *Jane Eyre* she wrote to her close friend, "If I <u>could</u> leave home Ellen—I should not be at Haworth now." What keeps her at home are her duties and obligations to her father. She has bowed her head to the poet Southey's dictatorial advice and has accepted her "proper duties." Brontë has chained herself—through love and tenderness—to a domestic life she longs to leave. But the secret inner life of passionate engagement still calls. Even as a few lines later in the same letter, censuring herself in oblique language Ellen may not have understood, Brontë acknowledges that she had yielded to "an eager desire for release" and had returned to Brussels after her aunt's death against her conscience, driven by "an irresistible impulse." Now she realizes that she has been punished by two years empty of either happiness or peace. Her father's early warning seems to have proved true. So through yet another wish-fulfillment in her fiction, Brontë lets Jane do what she cannot: run away— guilty, yes, of abandoning *her* master and weeping scalding tears— yet doing what *she* chooses. Charlotte's letter in the same paragraph voices her darkest fears about the consequences of staying. She feels that "life is passing away" and bleakly foresees that when she's finally free she may not be able to find employment. Now past the prime of life her "faculties will be rusted." Still, her "Conscience . . . affirms that I am doing right in staying at home." For Jane too, conscience affirms something, but in her case that she must leave. Charlotte, writing these conflicted pages, understands both her own wish to leave and her need to stay. Fixed as she is in Haworth, writing her novel in secret, she must find a way out for both her heroine and herself. This begins with Jane's abandonment of self into the wild, which, in many ways, corresponds to her inner life. Bleak, vacant, desolate.

Thus, Jane Eyre finds herself two days later on a summer evening destitute, divorced from any tie with human society, absolutely alone. She is standing by a stone pillar. All around her are the great moors where the heather grows deep and wild, and four white, empty roads stretch out broad and lonely toward unknown distances. Charlotte Brontë knew this place from her own experience. She had lived some of the most vivid moments of her life in scenes just like this. Her sister Emily repeatedly used this same signpost in *Wuthering Heights* as an emblem of isolation and choice. Now Jane Eyre, who has never known a mother's love and has no one to turn to, decides in her solitude to turn to "the universal Mother, Nature" resolving to "seek her breast and ask repose." Finding a place to hide, a womb-shaped hollow deeply furrowing the brown moor side, she feels that "Nature is benign and good" and that "she loved me, outcast as I was." Being now a woman who could only expect from other people "mistrust, rejection, insult," she clings to nature with filial fondness.

Charlotte Brontë recalls in these pages her childhood when, having lost her mother Maria, she turned to the moors, which stretched for seemingly limitless miles beyond the Haworth parsonage as a place of freedom, delight, and security. Ellen Nussey, who visited there in 1833, was later to remember the interplay of place and emotion vividly alive in all the Brontës. It seemed to her as if they did not live " 'in' " the house, except for eating, drinking, and resting. Instead, they lived in the free expanse of moorland, with its purple heather, its dells and glens and brooks, delighting in the beauty and the isolation, sharing a seclusion enjoyed by "intelligent companionship and intense family affection." It is the highly personal character of these experiences Brontë is remembering. The moors were a strange, new territory for Jane. She had lived within the sometimes imprisoning, sometimes sheltering confines of Gateshead, Lowood, and Thornfield. Nevertheless Jane seems to trust in the notion of nature as Mother, so instinctive and natural to Charlotte, unaware of the dangers that face the lonely individual cut off from the supportive society of family and friends.

Charlotte was to say of her sister Emily what was exactly true for herself as well: she "loved the moors." For both, flowers "brighter than the rose bloomed in the blackest of the heath." Their minds could "make an Eden" out of the sullen hollow in a livid hillside. Both found in this bleak solitude many delights, and "not the least and best-loved was—liberty." In later years, the Brontës continued to wander freely. Remembering her time with them, Ellen writes of delightful rambles on the moors and down into the glens and ravines. There was always "a <u>lingering</u> delight" in these spots. Every moss, every flower, every tint and form, were noted and enjoyed. Emily and Anne would lead to a place they called the "Meeting of the Waters" It was a small oasis of emerald green turf broken here and there by small clear springs. Seated there, "we were hidden from all the world," with nothing to see but miles and miles of heather. So blissful could these memories be, that in *Wuthering Heights* Emily Brontë gives her heroine Catherine Earnshaw this dream: She has died and is in heaven, but she is not happy; "heaven did not seem to be my home; and I broke my heart with weeping to come back to earth; and the angels were so angry that they flung me out into the middle of the heath on the top of Wuthering Heights; where I woke sobbing for joy." The novel's narrator, Lockwood, seems to implicitly understand. In its last lines he visits Catherine's grave site, lying next to those of Edgar Linton and Heathcliff, and tells us that he lingers under "that benign sky" watching the moths flutter, listening to the soft wind breathing through the grass. And he wonders "how any one could ever imagine unquiet slumbers for the sleepers in that quiet earth." There is no need for another heaven.

But Jane wakes the next morning hungry. With a rude suddenness she realizes that the moor is in fact "a golden desert." And she as a human being "had a human being's wants." What follows are some of Jane Eyre's most painful days. Her father's poetry anticipated the outcome that Charlotte Brontë now so carefully develops.

> But Summer's gone, and Winter here,
> With iron scepter rules the year—
> Beneath this dark inclement sky,
> How many wanderers faint and die!

In his "Winter—Night Meditations," Patrick depicts the dangers of the moors when the weather changes and suddenly death threatens. It is this dark turn of fortune Charlotte finds necessary. Though happy to return to memories of childhood pleasures in the moors, she now drives home the point that nature is not a mother; that mother, like Maria Brontë, is no longer there to nurture and protect her solitary daughter.

⬥

"Hopeless of the future," Jane Eyre wishes to die so that she might be absolved by death from further conflict with fate. In this despairing moment, she imagines her body decaying quietly, mingling "in peace with the soil of this wilderness."

Charlotte may have longed to run away while writing *Jane Eyre* to escape vicariously with Jane; her brother Branwell chose a different method of fleeing his problems. Regarding his forced separation from Mrs. Robinson as the consequence of a malign "fate," he had already begun the self-abusive conduct that would lead to his early death. In his powerful poem "Penmaenmawr," written in 1845, Branwell compares his despairing self "defenseless against human ill," the victim of "ceaseless strife and change," to the grim, black sublimity of the Welsh mountain, claiming a kind of kinship for his "heart worn down by care."

There is a kind of literary model or antecedents for all this. Branwell several years earlier had discovered a strange novel, the *Private Memoires and Confessions of a Justified Sinner* (1824) by the Scotch writer James Hogg, who was for many years a regular contributor to *Blackwood's Edinburgh Magazine*. Both Branwell and Charlotte became fascinated by the tragic course of its protagonist who thinks he is being pursued by a devil named Gil-Martin who has tricked him into murdering his brother. He calls Gil-Martin "Master." Flight into the countryside does not enable him to escape this persecutor, and in his diary he writes in despair, in words that anticipate Jane's, "My body being quite exhausted by suffering, I am grown weak and feeble." He pictures himself, in language closely similar to Charlotte's and to Branwell's, as "the child of earthly misery and despair." All that is left for him is to "wish myself in my grave every hour of the day." Abandoning hope, this tragic figure hangs himself, and the local people bury him on a hillside, his suicide preventing his being interred in sacred ground. Branwell was drawn to this melodramatic precedent, and at first Jane Eyre is tempted to do the same. But she has to admit, in terms typical of Charlotte's religiously inflected thinking and its strong sense of duty, that her life is "one of my possessions; with all its requirements, and pains, and responsibilities."

Driven by hunger, Jane begins to wander, choosing, for no particular reason, to walk down one of the four roads leading from the white pillar, while "apathy" clogs her heart. What follows is a series of remarkable scenes in which Brontë imagines what it must be like to be an outcast begging for work, for food, even for just a word of kindness. Jane wanders into villages, asking if there are any jobs available, trying to exchange her scarf or her gloves for a roll, "gnawed by nature's cravings." One of her difficulties is that her "character, position, tale" seem "doubtful" because she is dressed and acts like a middle-class woman and not a beggar. She finds it difficult to ask for help because she is "seized with shame." At one point she approaches a parsonage, thinking it is the clergyman's function to help, and is met with cold indifference by a servant. "Again," she tells us, "I crawled away." Later an old servant blocking a doorway tells her, "You should not be roving about now; it looks very ill." Why do these simple, local people find her suspicious? What can they think she is guilty of?

Charlotte Brontë drew upon her experiences in her imaginative construction of Jane's dreadful wandering.

First, as a witness. In November of 1840 the wife of a local curate came to the door of the Haworth parsonage seeking advice and help from Charlotte's father Patrick. This was Mrs. Collins, coming to tell "a most melancholy tale of her wretched husband's drunken, extravagant, profligate habits," as Charlotte informed Ellen Nussey in a letter. The woman saw no future possibilities for herself—"there was nothing, she said, but ruin before them." It was clear her husband was about to be expelled from his clerical duties because "his vices were utterly hopeless." Her painful admission was that her husband treated her and her child "savagely." Patrick's advice was to leave him at once. Where she might go, what she might do, are not at all clear given the isolation of the small towns and villages in the West Riding of Yorkshire. Thinking over this tragic story, Charlotte wonders how Mrs. Collins ever got herself into this situation. She writes that she is "morally certain" that "no decent woman" could experience anything but aversion toward such a man, and she insists that from her first meeting Collins, she had instinctively hated him. Charlotte seems to blame Mrs. Collins for bad judgment, implying she too should have recognized from the start things would go poorly. Mrs. Collins seems to be guilty for what happened.

There are elements to this situation that Charlotte was to replicate six years later as she wrote *Jane Eyre*. While it would be a mistake to push the parallel to an extreme, it is the case that Mr. Rochester too was, at least, emotionally abusive at times to Bertha, Céline, and even Jane. His sometimes angry temper and sexual appetite had, before Jane met him, damaged him, and during the action of the novel he does everything he can to persuade or force Jane into what she considers an illicit relationship, one she in the end must escape, much like Mrs. Collins, at the risk of her life. Penniless, homeless, without family or friends, beginning to starve to death, an "object of suspicion" as a "well-dressed beggar," and in this respect perhaps even looking like Mrs. Collins, Jane seems to others unworthy of sympathy or help. She internalizes and accepts their suspicion and rejection. Quite unfairly, as in the case of Mrs. Collins, Jane feels a "moral degradation, blent with physical suffering" that "form too distressing a recollection ever to be willingly dwelt upon." She accepts the role of abjection, expelled from acceptable society because an aspect of her past has made her guilty.

Charlotte also had a more personal experience of desperate alienation one summer in Brussels, painful memories of which emerge in Jane Eyre's wandering. In the summer of 1843 Charlotte had largely ceased her studies with Constantin and was again in the unhappy role of teacher for students she intensely disliked. And then the long summer holidays began, and all the students and the other teachers, save one, were gone. Charlotte found herself alone: "I have nobody to speak to—for I count the Belgians as nothing." In her solitude she would wander from room to room in the pensionnat Heger finding that the silence and loneliness of the house "weight down one's spirits like lead." Everything about this experience anticipates Jane's wandering: the emptiness, the hostility to anyone she encounters, the gathering depression, the helplessness. By August, Charlotte finds that "Earth and Heaven seem dreary and empty to me." Like Mrs. Collins, and in anticipation of Jane Eyre, she too has a painful memory of baffled love and expulsion with which she must live. In one letter she notes Mme. Heger's coldness toward her, and she confesses to Ellen, "I fancy I begin to perceive the reason of this . . . ," which at times make her "laugh and & other times nearly cry." It's not at all difficult to infer that Heger's chilly demeanor is because she suspects that this bright and favored student of her husband has begun to harbor feelings for him that are a danger to them all. Charlotte in Brussels in 1843, like Jane Eyre wandering starving through isolated Yorkshire villages, has a bitter story that she cannot tell, which leaves her pleading with Ellen to write back and "comfort a very desolate heart."

Indeed the solitude, sense of desertion, as well as feelings of secret, hidden guilt, led Charlotte to wandering, just as Jane was to do, to assuage her unhappiness. By September she writes, "I have tramped about a good deal." In trying to protect herself from falling "into the gulf of low spirits" she would wander the boulevards and streets of Brussels sometimes for hours. Even the city fails to help after a while. And so she hikes out of town to the Protestant cemetery and looks beyond, seeing "nothing but fields as far as the horizon." Here, we are very close to Jane's experiences. In Charlotte's letter she notes that she feels a repulsion to returning to the school "which contained nothing I cared for," and so she wanders through the streets to avoid it. The absence of anyone to "care for" is surely an oblique reference to the prohibition she now feels in her caring for M. Heger. So troubled was Charlotte by her conflicted feelings of abandonment and guilt over her illicit desires that one afternoon this intensely anti-Catholic woman actually went inside the church of Ste. Gudule and entered a confessional. The priest opened the grill to permit her to speak, and she didn't know how to begin. Later she was to tell Ellen Nussey, "I actually did confess - a real confession." The real confession solved nothing. The guilt remained and her problems continued. The priest urged her to come to him for lessons in the Catholic faith, but of course she never did. Not having, as Mrs. Collins did, the sympathetic attention of the Rev. Patrick Brontë, Charlotte needed but could not turn to someone satisfactory for help during this crisis.

Even after the return of the students and the recommencement of her teaching duties, Charlotte could not shake off the kind of "apathy" that Jane Eyre later feels. In October, still she was "completely alone" and observed: "It is a curious position to be so utterly solitary in the midst of numbers—sometimes this solitude oppresses me to an excess."

⁂

Mrs. Collins returned to the Haworth parsonage in April 1847. By then Charlotte Brontë was making a fair copy of at least the first parts of *Jane Eyre*. She had echoed the woman's sufferings in Jane's. Now, she was to hear the happy ending of her story. Collins appeared at the door "pale and worn but still interesting looking and cleanly and neatly dressed," her little girl at her side. Charlotte served her tea and heard of her new life, "her activity and perseverance." She had "triumphed over the hideous disease"—almost certainly syphilis forced on her by her husband—and had regained "a decent position in society," running her own lodging house in a respectable part of the suburbs of Manchester "and is doing very well." Mr. Collins has disappeared, and of course she "can never more endure to see him."

A successful escape. And a very proto-feminist one. Now, Charlotte's novel turns to imagining similar happiness for Jane Eyre.

Perfect Congeniality

During the 1840s Charlotte Brontë sometimes felt a restless desire to leave Haworth. However, far more typical and persistent are her contrary feelings of love and intimate connection with home. During her months threading the lonely streets of Brussels, they became particularly intense. Brontë describes what she misses in a remarkable testimonial sent to Emily in October 1843. It's written on a Sunday, and all the participants in the pensionnat Heger are at what she calls "their idolatrous 'Messe.'" Sitting alone in the refectory, Charlotte is reminded of the kitchen at Haworth. She pictures herself there, "cutting up hash" with Emily who is standing by watching that she put in enough flour and not too much pepper. The pet cat Tiger is "jumping about the dish and carving-knife," while Emily's favorite pet dog Keeper "stands like a devouring flame on the kitchen-floor" as both wait for Charlotte to toss them the best fragments of mutton. Tabby, their nickname for the now elderly family servant, is blowing the fire to boil potatoes into "a sort of vegetable glue!" These are, for Charlotte, "divine . . . recollections." There is something heavenly about this for her. Haworth and the Yorkshire moors are a kind of Brontaëan paradise. Wistfully Charlotte continues, admitting that while Brussels is "dismal to me," she doesn't feel free to return home without a fixed prospect of something to do, and she asks Emily whether she and "Papa" really want her to come home. Her need to be forgiven for the distance she has put between herself and her family is palpable.

What Charlotte loves, what she yearns for, what is in a very particular way "divine," are the simple details of ordinary life—household chores, the ever present pets, Tabby loved despite, or perhaps even because, of her bad cooking, a part of her sweet and lifelong devotion to the Brontë children, who are now adults. Charlotte ends praying God's blessing upon "our grey half-inhabited house."

Readers interested in the Brontës—their fictions, their poetry, but more specifically their letters—soon become familiar with this small, ordinary, intensely loved world. You can see it in one peculiar form of record-keeping that became a habit for Emily and Anne, the so-called "Diary Papers." Every four years they would sit down on their birthdays and write brief descriptions of the day, short lists of recent events, and speculations about the future. The page would then be folded up so it would be as tiny as a sixpence and put into a tin box. Four years later it was to be opened. A delightful example is Emily's of November 24, 1834. It's her sixteenth birthday. Charlotte was then eighteen. Emily has just fed the cats Rainbow, Diamond, and Snowflake as well as a pheasant named Jasper. Branwell arrives, announcing he has heard that Sir Robert Peel will stand for Leeds. Emily and Anne have been peeling apples for Charlotte to make apple pudding. Tabby wants them to peel some potatoes as well. The rather stern Aunt Branwell pops in to ask Emily if she's sitting properly with her feet on the floor. Sally Mosley is washing up in the back kitchen. Emily confesses she has not tidied up her bedroom or done her lessons, but still she wants to go out to play. And she hasn't done her piano practicing yet. Dinner is going to be boiled beef, turnips, potatoes, and apple pudding. Emily takes up a knife and begins peeling potatoes. Stuck in the middle of all this is a note: "The Gondals are . . . discovering the interior of Gaaldine." This is a reference to the fantasy narratives Emily and Anne are writing. The casual interpolation of the remark illustrates how real and strangely ordinary for Emily are the developments in that world as well as in this one. Perhaps this quaint page might delight readers simply for its snapshot of a Yorkshire parsonage kitchen in November of 1834, but it acquires far greater significance when we consider it's by the future author of *Wuthering Heights*. Home, and a very specific and particular home, is thus the object of desire for both Emily and Charlotte Brontë; the place where they have known the greatest happiness, and the place their characters long for.

Charlotte voiced this yearning during her exile in Brussels in her evidently autobiographical poem "The Teacher's Monologue." On a tranquil evening, the speaker, alienated in the "strange, coarse world" where she must work, and for the present moment alone, "still and untroubled," remembers a home "where I am known and loved." Both morning and evening she feels a changeless yearning for that other place. She recalls her happiest hours, lived among moors, before her life decayed into "dark anxiety." The antithesis between her unhappy present contrasting with memories of her happy past provokes fear of the future. What if distant family members die? What if the home becomes empty? "What shall I do, and whither turn?" These thoughts and feelings from her long stay in

Brussels lingered in Charlotte Brontë's mind when she began writing *Jane Eyre*; indeed, they had become a constant in her thinking.

When Charlotte returned to Haworth in January of 1844, it was to a home far more troubled than the childhood closeness described in Emily's 1834 Diary Paper. The parsonage had really become "our grey half-inhabited house." Anne and Branwell were away as governess and tutor at Thorpe Green. Mr. Brontë's eyesight was failing. Worse still, in the years to follow the home became haunted by the twin specters of "Sin and Suffering"—her father's illness, her brother's despair and self-destruction. This is the home Charlotte now sometimes wants to leave. But for what? She can never return to the place she most longs for: the same home, not as it is now, but rather as she remembers it from earlier, happier years. So at times, as it seems to the unhappy teacher in her poem, she despairs that this home may be "but a dream," nothing more than "sweet thoughts I live on" that all too soon seem to "vanish into vacancy."

Where could Charlotte Brontë escape to? Well, one of her solutions was, through a novel, to bring Jane Eyre to the place Charlotte yearned for and to make those evanescent "sweet thoughts" real again through an imaginative reconstruction of the Haworth of her greatest happiness. Brontë makes that place of her own, earlier remembered happiness Jane's refuge. The destination for her brave and stalwart heroine, who like Odysseus and Aeneas, Swift's Gulliver and Bunyan's Christian, works through challenges and tribulations to reach a home, one that, importantly, Jane has never known, but which is at the same time a home that has always been hers in not only an instinctive but also ultimately, as we are about to see, in a strangely, deeply rooted way. In these chapters *Jane Eyre* thus continues to be a richly autobiographical novel. Though for as long as she was able, Charlotte Brontë maintained the illusion that it was not.

Jane finds a home, a family, financial security, and independence. Brontë uses the factual details of things that indeed had happened, and that were still present in her happy memories, transforming them into the fictive experience of Jane Eyre. In this way she is able through imagination to return to a Haworth purged of unhappiness, redolent of the "sweet thoughts I live on . . ."

The home Jane reaches through the rain is named for its location, Marsh End/Moor House. Much like the Haworth parsonage, it is solitary, at a distance from the village, and located just at the edge of the moors. Jane, desperate with exhaustion, peering through a small window sees a humble kitchen and an elderly woman, somewhat rough-looking but scrupulously clean, knitting a stocking. The servant, Hannah, resembles the Brontë's loyal old Tabby, and both speak in Yorkshire dialect, calling, for example, the grown women of the family "childer." As Ellen Nussey remembered from her 1833 visit to the parsonage, "We were all 'Childer' and 'Bairns' in her estimation." Hannah's vigilance at the door this evening replicates Tabby's vigilance "jealously seizing" the daily post deliveries at the Haworth front door and carrying them off, as Ellen later remembers, "with hobbling step and shaking hand" to be delivered directly to Charlotte. Hannah's efforts to keep Jane Eyre out this evening—"You should not be roving about now; it looks very ill."—are exactly what Tabby would do. Her knitting, and, in later kitchen scenes, her baking bread and pies were Tabby's daily chores.

Patrick Brontë's chronic fear of fire meant that Haworth had no drapes and only two carpets—most of the home had sanded stone floors—as Ellen noted always clean—as here at Moor House. The parlor is furnished much like the one in Haworth, with no superfluous ornaments and not one modern piece of furniture, save a brace of work-boxes and a lady's desk in rosewood. A desk much like Charlotte's.

But what most importantly strikes Jane Eyre, in this first glimpse through the window, are two young women who resemble her. They too are "pale and grave," thoughtful almost to severity, "all delicacy and cultivation." Instinctively she seems intimate with every lineament of their appearance. As indeed she should be, since though she doesn't know it at the time, these are her cousins, their mother the sister of Jane's father. They look like her. And though the novel does not say it, they look very much like Charlotte Brontë and her sisters.

Immediately Jane recognizes their minds and their values are hers as well. Diana and Maria are at the moment intent on translating a German tale and discussing how Franz tells Daniel about a dream from which he has awakened in terror. One responds: "That is strong . . . I relish it." Emily and Charlotte had studied German in Brussels. They, too, have for many years been interested in the unconscious, and their novels feature strange and unnerving dreams—that they relished. Their aim, as is the aim of the Rivers sisters, had been to prepare themselves to open up their own school. Both the Brontës and the sisters Rivers have been forced to work as governesses, in families, by whose "wealthy and haughty" members, as Jane puts it, they were regarded as humble dependents. Opening a school looks like an escape. Jane Eyre, peering through the window sees not only cousins—she sees versions of Emily and Anne in a typical evening's occupation at Haworth.

Brontë is clear on what has led Jane to this moment: "Sympathies." Jane explains earlier in the novel, defining one of its crucial concepts, "Sympathies, I believe, exist: (for instance, between far-

distant, long-absent, wholly estranged relatives; asserting, notwith-
standing their alienation, the unity of the source to which each traces
his origin)," and she acknowledges that the working of such extraordinary moments of instinctive connection "baffle mortal comprehen-
sion." Charlotte had for many years delighted in stories that featured
inexplicable "sympathies" that she read in Aunt Branwell's complete
set of the *Methodist Magazine*, which she characterizes in her later
novel *Shirley* as "full of miracles and apparitions, of preternatural
warnings, ominous dreams." While to some readers it might be difficult to believe that Jane Eyre, fleeing Rochester, could get into a
coach going she knows not where; wander through what was for her
a completely unknown area of Yorkshire; and finally, thanks to the
tiny light of a solitary candle glimpsed through the rain in the gathering night, come upon her only living relatives who are uncannily like
her in almost every respect, to Charlotte Brontë this is simply a result
of the inexorable attraction of genetic and psychic sympathies drawing Jane home. Her actual, real home. A home she has never known
but has been destined to reach. And a place that is also Charlotte
Brontë's idealized home. The names of the two cousins are key. The
older cousin, Diana, is named for the Greek goddess of the moon,
protector of innocent women and herself virgin. In Brontë's novel, as
we have seen, she appears in crucial scenes from those depicting Miss
Temple at Lowood school to Jane's dream the night before she flees
Thornfield. Consistently the moon suggests a protective female spirit
watching over Jane's arduous destiny. The younger cousin, Mary,
takes the name of Charlotte's mother, eldest sister, and Jane's guiding
teacher Maria Temple. These women have been deeply linked to both
Charlotte Brontë and Jane Eyre throughout their lives.

In the days that follow her recovery to health, the Rivers family—
including St. John, the brother, who admits Jane on that first

evening—accepts her as one of their own. She is eager to help Hannah in the kitchen picking over gooseberries for a pie and is soon sharing in discussions about books and ideas in the parlor. This balancing of household chores with a shared and intense intellectual development had been familiar to Charlotte since her childhood. The young Brontë girls had been trained by their Aunt Branwell in needlework and prided themselves on their skill in sewing silk, "turning" old clothes to be reused, and mending. They made sheets, bolster-cases, towels, and every article of female apparel. On a daily basis they made their own beds, swept and cleaned the house, and helped with the cooking. In later years when Tabby became infirm, it was Emily who made all the bread for the family; and anyone passing by the kitchen door, as Elizabeth Gaskell recalled, might have seen her studying German from an open book, propped up before her, "as she kneaded the dough." By 1839 Charlotte had admitted that to others the Brontës might seem "odd animals." However, she notes, "Human feelings are queer things— I am much happier—black-leading the stoves—making the beds and sweeping the floors at home, than I should be living like a fine lady anywhere else."

During her first glimpse of Diana and Mary, Jane notes an old pointer dog is resting his massive head on one girl's knee, while a black cat rests in the other's lap. The Brontës loved and named their pets, many living in the parsonage itself. Emily's Diary Paper for July 1841, typically, includes references to two tamed geese, Victoria and Adelaide—whimsically named after the queen and her aunt— her current favorite dog Keeper, and Nero, probably a hawk kept in a cage. If Charlotte confesses that she and her siblings are odd animals, they had, always, sympathy for other living creatures and sensed a kinship with them too.

The parsonage garden at Haworth was nearly all grass, with a few stunted shrubs and currant bushes. Similarly, the garden at Moor House has few flowers, and those only of the hardiest species. The Brontës never seem to have been interested in gardening. After all, paces from their door there were miles of moorland, and the Rivers would seem to agree.

On that first night, the Rivers family gathers around Jane, who looks thin, bloodless, almost like a specter. Quite reasonably, they begin to question her—Can they get in touch with friends? How can they help her? She invents an alias, Jane Elliott. As she begins to get warm, to take a little something to eat, she tells us that she begins to again "know myself."

That Jane wishes to keep her identity secret to conceal her flight from Mr. Rochester makes sense, but it is intriguing that as she does this she begins to feel more herself. Jane seems to find the use of an alias, keeping her past life and experiences secret from these kindly people, makes her not only more herself, it also, in fact, makes her more akin to the Charlotte Brontë who is inventing her. We have seen how Charlotte and Branwell used pseudonymous narrators for much of their juvenilia. Similarly, in a very curious and revealing moment, Charlotte wrote to Hartley Coleridge, son of the famous poet and himself a literary man, in December of 1840, sending him some of her writing and asking his opinion. She makes much of the fact that she has playfully not told him her gender and expresses pleasure that he has not been able to figure out whether she is a woman or a man—"the soft or the hard sex" as she rather coyly puts it. As she closes she expresses her gratitude that he has been kind to "an anonymous scribe who had not even the manners to tell you whether . . . his common-place 'C T' meant Charles Tims or Charlotte Tomkins." The teasing manner of her writing—which goes on at some length and is full of allusions to other writers and to periodicals of past decades—suggests the pleasure she is having in maintaining the secret of her identity. Charlotte and her sisters carried on this same kind of deception in the publication of their poems and novels, just as Branwell used the pseudonym Northangerland when his poems appeared in provincial newspapers in the last years of his brief life. This is the Brontëan paradox: they feel far more themselves adopting names and sometimes roles quite different from who they actually were. Jane, at this moment, is quite like them.

Jane Eyre soon becomes the new member of the family community, experiencing what she describes as pleasure arising from "perfect congeniality of taste, sentiments, and principles." Diana, in sharing these feelings, tells Jane, "at home we like to be free, even to licence," voicing a keen sense for the liberty that Charlotte and Emily had felt wandering the moors. Jane now learns, for the first time in her life, this same delight in the "swell and sweep" of the landscape, of it loneliness, its colors, and its changeable lights during different times of the day. Soon she is under its "spell," which has already and for so long entranced her new found friends, just as for many years it had entranced Charlotte Brontë.

Jane likes to sit on a stool, with her head on Diana's knee, listening to the two sisters talk. Soon, Diana is teaching her German. In a remarkable moment, Jane uses the very same kind of language that Charlotte had used in describing her first months of study with Constantin Heger now adapting it to her cousin: "I liked to learn of her: I saw the part of instructress pleased and suited her; that of scholar please and suited me no less." It's as if Charlotte cannot forget that relationship and the sense of kinship it gave her, and so delights in creating echoes of it in her novel.

The uncanny sympathies that have drawn her to Moor House now intensify. If Charlotte has lost Heger and Jane has lost—at least for the moment—her Rochester, now they have found something else. A new family. "Our natures dovetailed: mutual affection—of the strongest kind—was the result." Jane too begins to teach, instructing a grateful Maria in drawing, a skill of which both Jane and Charlotte were proud. Maria in turn is a docile, assiduous pupil. The hours, the days, by. Charlotte Brontë returns to memories of her happiest years at Haworth when the brother and three sisters studied, played, and wrote together in a kind of sympathetic community intensified by the isolation of their lives. In a letter of 1841, written while she was governess to the Sidgwick family, Charlotte explains to Ellen Nussey's brother Henry, "my home is humble and unattractive to strangers" but is, to her, unlike any other place on earth, where she shared a "profound and intense affection" with siblings whose "minds are cast in the same mould, their ideas drawn from the same source." Charlotte as novelist now makes that kind of happiness live for her wandering orphan and in a way for herself as well.

And then she crowns that level of joy-filled contentment with something that she had never known: a fortune. Throughout *Jane Eyre,* Brontë threads hints of a rich Uncle Eyre somewhere to the south. He leaves Jane everything—twenty thousand pounds. In Chapter One we considered how anxieties about financial stability haunted the Brontës—and perhaps affected Charlotte, who characteristically as the eldest daughter felt the most responsibility for the family well-being, more than any of the others. The Rivers family had experienced similar anxieties, finding that on the recent death of their father they have little left. But with Jane's windfall, their concerns melt away. Jane will divide the money four ways. Their worries are at an end. And more to the point, for her, she can now affirm as fact what she had felt since the night of her arrival: She has found a brother and two sisters, what she celebrates as "wealth to the heart! . . . not like the ponderous gift of gold." She claps her hands with joy. Speaking from an authority that new-found wealth now gives her, she tells St. John, "I will have a home and connections." Imagining their shared future, she anticipates "delicious pleasure," confessing the "craving" she has for "fraternal and sisterly love." When St. John, who is already hatching plans of his own, asks if she doesn't harbor hopes of marrying someday, she insists she never will, and that what she wants is "my kindred"—with them she enjoys "full fellow feeling."

At this moment the novel echoes themes from an important, indeed revelatory, letter written perhaps a year before Charlotte created these scenes, a letter that comes about two-and-a-half months after she has sent her last, desperate message to M. Heger. It's addressed to Miss Wooler, Charlotte's old and trusted teacher and later employer at Roe Head.

Her first topic is money. The Brontë sisters have invested much of what little they have in railroad shares, and recently there has been an investor panic and some people have lost everything. Charlotte is anxious to sell, but her sisters don't wish to—Emily in particular. Charlotte is ready to yield to her views valuing a sister's judgement because of their shared affection for each other. Just as with Jane Eyre later on, Charlotte thinks family love and mutual sympathy take precedence over financial matters.

She goes on to worry about Branwell. The faculty of "self-government" she fears, is completely lost in him. She remarks, "men are strange beings . . ." and wonders at the way her society permits boys to take risks never permitted to young women, finding her brother a sad example of this unreasonable gender inequality. Why shouldn't women, who demonstrate self-government, be rewarded for their discipline? She celebrates the "retributive justice" that has awarded Miss Wooler with a good life earned by work and self-denial, and notes that she has been speculating on possible happiness for "a lone woman." She has reached the point of considering that there is "no more respectable character on this earth than an u[n]married woman who makes her own way through life."

At the moment in *Jane Eyre* when her heroine receives a fortune, gives three-quarters of it away to her cousins—whom she repeatedly calls sisters and brother—and joyfully asserts she doesn't wish to marry but rather to enjoy the fellow-feeling of her kindred, Jane seems to enact Charlotte's values regarding money, family, and happiness. If Jane still thinks of the Mr. Rochester she has lost—and she does—so too does Charlotte think of M. Heger. But she's finding a way to move on, to be a respectable, unmarried, and happy woman.

To affirm all of this, there now come the Christmas scenes. December holidays had been precious to Charlotte for many reasons. In recent years they had meant liberation from her duties as teacher or governess, a time when family members gathered at Haworth to reconstitute their small society and the pleasures of the past. So now, enabled by her new wealth, Jane reopens the recently deserted Moor House and with Hannah begins to *"clean down"* the place, polishing, arranging, cooking, and generally getting all ready for the return of Diana and Mary. St. John, ever the insensitive and serious one, faults her, insisting she "look a little higher than domestic endearments and household joys."

Jane's reply is the climactic conclusion to this whole section of the novel: these kinds of happiness are "[t]he best things the world has!"

⁂

St. John Rivers' challenge to Jane Eyre's love for home is prompted by his eagerness to make her his wife and take her with him when he travels to British India as a missionary.

When they first meet he is, by his own account, only "the incumbent of a poor country parish," who sacrifices himself for the sake of his flock. Bad weather or lengthy distances never keep him from visiting the sick and poor. But he is not content. As Jane gets to know him better, he admits that he is an ambitious man and he confesses to her, "I . . . almost rave in my restlessness."

In Rivers Brontë creates a second suitor for Jane who is as different as possible from Mr. Rochester. Fair-haired, blue-eyed, with colorless white skin like ivory and a profile like a Greek statue, he is a veritable Apollo. St. John, while reservedly affectionate to his sisters, always distances himself from them and from their intensifying relationship with Jane. He finds in Jane not a kindred spirit who inflames his passion, but the plain and sober helpmate he wants for what he considers a glorious life as a soldier for Christ. She finally agrees she will come with him as an assistant, but she refuses to accept the loveless marriage he offers. St. John finds this insulting and impractical. He will take her only on his terms.

Charlotte Brontë didn't know anyone much like this character, who is perhaps the most fully invented person in *Jane Eyre*. However, she certainly knew clergymen, and there are suggestive aspects of her past that Charlotte wove together to fashion at least aspects of this strange man.

The small world of provincial Anglican clergy, of which Patrick Brontë and his children were a part, consisted of the incumbents, that is, priests appointed to specific parishes, and curates, recently ordained young men who assisted the incumbents until they obtained parishes of their own. It was assumed that the daughters of incumbents would be suitable matches for these young men, and as Patrick Brontë's oldest daughter, Charlotte was, as it were, first in line for a proposal should one come along. This was a situation she didn't like at all. Hence when Henry Nussey, brother to her good friend Ellen, sent a cool, reasoned letter to Charlotte proposing marriage early in March of 1839, suggesting that as his wife she might run a local parish school, he was acting very much as their world expected. Charlotte's polite but decided rejection characterized the kind of woman who would be a good mate for him as mild and pious, with steady, cheerful spirits. Indeed, the kind of woman St. John Rivers would need for his work in India. Charlotte, however, sees herself as "romantic," "eccentric," "satirical," and wrong for him. She rejects any implication that to avoid "the stigma of old maid" she would marry a worthy man she cannot hope to make "happy" and who would certainly not make her happy. In a letter sent to Ellen seven days later she explained her decision, declaring that for her marriage must be based upon an "intense attachment" to a man. And she adds, repeating her earlier letter to Henry, that he would think her "a wild, romantic enthusiast" who would "laugh and satirize and say whatever came into my head first." It's exactly this volatile, free spirit that later surprises and disturbs St. John Rivers when he sees it in Jane Eyre.

Interestingly, Henry had, nine years earlier, written in his diary that if it was in God's will, he would accept the calling to be a missionary. When Charlotte learned of this ambition, which Henry soon abandoned, she wrote Ellen, characterizing his notion as "amusing" and sardonically remarking that "he would not live a year" in the hostile climates of those countries where missionaries were needed. Certainly the memory of this lingered and helped contribute to Charlotte's St. John Rivers.

While Charlotte did turn Henry Nussey down in 1839, there was an element of regret because, as the brother of one of Charlotte's dearest friends, marriage to Henry might have led to a household in which her friend would also live. This was, in her own peculiar words, "a strong temptation," and she conceded, "I thought if I were to marry so, Ellen could live with me and how happy I should be." As she wrote these lines surely both she and Ellen recalled an earlier letter of September 1836 that Charlotte closes in this way: "Ellen I wish I could live with you always." She continues, "I begin to cling to you more fondly than ever I did." This is her dream: "If we had but a cottage and a competency of our own I do think we might live and love on till <u>Death</u> . . ." needing no one else. This declaration, written at the age of twenty when Charlotte was teaching at Miss Wooler's school in Roe Head, is remarkable. While there is little to suggest that Brontë was consciously expressing same-sex affection and desire for Ellen, there is no escaping the "until death do us part" of the traditional marriage ritual she knew well, nor terms such as "fond" and "clinging." At the very least, in this early letter Charlotte is already imagining the kind of sisterhood that she later evokes in describing Jane Eyre's idyllic communal life at Moor House, and the economic independence she was to praise in considering the life of Miss Wooler.

Other clergymen then came into her life. Instinctively, it would seem, Charlotte disliked them all. In August 1839 a dashing young graduate from Durham, William Weightman, arrived at Haworth as Patrick's curate. Charlotte found him "very fickle" and a "thorough male-flirt." When he learned that none of the Brontë girls had ever received a valentine, he walked ten miles to a nearby town to post each of them an anonymous poem. His tenure was cruelly cut short. Visiting a parish resident, Weightman became infected with cholera and died during that tragic year of 1842.

Three years later, in May of 1845, A. B. Nicholls, a shy, robust man from the north of Ireland arrived as Patrick's new curate. Soon, the rumors began and Charlotte treated them with disdain. "A cold far-away sort of civility," she wrote, "are the only terms on which I have ever been with Mr. Nicholls." She continued, in a characteristically waspish tone, that he and his fellow curates "regard me as an old maid, and I regard them, one and all, as highly uninteresting, narrow and unattractive specimens of the 'coarser sex.'"

The asperity here, which spills over into her characterization of St. John Rivers in chapters from *Jane Eyre* written just a few months later, may have been exacerbated by an important holiday visit from the preceding July. Ellen Nussey and Charlotte had visited Ellen's brother and Charlotte's former suitor Henry, now the incumbent at a nearby town, Hathersage. He had married, in May, a woman from a wealthy family and was busy remodeling the parsonage before the happy couple moved in. Ellen and Charlotte's visit was partly to make suggestions about this project. During their stay Charlotte was forced to confront what she had lost in turning Henry down, and her feelings, judging by Jane's experiences at Moor House, must have been a complicated mingling of regret and a sparring justification for her decision.

When she came to imagining St. John Rivers she transmuted all of this—Henry's feckless youthful ambitions, now long set aside, to be a missionary, Weightman's light-hearted flirtatiousness cut short, Nicholls as the most recent plausible possibility—into a man more their opposite than their reflection, giving to him the rigidity and ruthlessness that Jane Eyre finds frightening but also compelling.

That all these matters were of great importance to Charlotte Brontë clearly emerges in poems she published on these themes in May of 1846, just months before she commenced writing *Jane Eyre*.

In "Preference," a woman rejects a man's marriage proposal insisting she does not love him—exactly in the terms in which

Charlotte first rejected Henry Nussey—and when he reproaches her for coldness she responds, as Jane does to Rivers' demands she marry him, "My good-will is sisterly," and she defies his anger, as Jane was to with Rivers, "Rave not, rage not, wrath is fruitless, / Fury cannot change my mind."

A second poem, "The Missionary," anticipates still further, related themes. In *Jane Eyre*, St. John Rivers must repress his powerful sexual attraction for Rosamond Oliver, the pretty daughter of a local factory owner. In one telling scene, Jane watches St. John closely as Rosamond flirts with him. He has withdrawn his eyes from her and, looking down to a tuft of daisies, "he crushed the snowy heads of the closed flowers with his foot." Clearly he is repressing his strong desire for Rosamond. His preference for Jane is based upon his presumption she would be a helpmate, not a lover, though Jane understands that marrying him she would be forced to "endure all the forms of love (which I doubt not he would scrupulously observe)." In "The Missionary" the same kind of man speaks of forsaking his home, taking up fearful challenges, and necessarily renouncing with "soul-felt pain" what he "wildly" wishes to retain, and he addresses the woman he is abandoning exactly as Rivers would address Rosamond, if he were to let himself say what he feels, remembering when "my heart most for thy heart burned." Like Rivers, this future missionary feels compelled to take up "the glorious task" that he thinks is "for the progress of our race." One wonders to what degree these boasts about British imperialism are, in Brontë's rendering, ironic. Certainly *Jane Eyre* makes clear that Rivers lacks "that mental serenity, that inward content" she assumes should be a consequence of "sincere Christian" belief. Instead, in his Sunday sermon, what Jane hears reveals "troubling impulses of insatiate yearnings and disquieting aspirations." What he seeks in India is a kind of vainglory, soon followed by death.

A third poem from this 1846 collection anticipates the dramatic end to Rivers' efforts to master Jane's will—that key term that Jane again uses to describe his efforts to dominate her. "Apostacy" describes a woman on her deathbed rejecting the religious demands of a Roman Catholic clergyman: "Point not to thy Madonna, Priest,— / Thy sightless saint of stone," she cries defiantly. She has put her faith in her earthly love for a man, and " 'Tis my religion thus to love." In her last moments she hears his voice, springs up, and falls back dead.

Jane Eyre exactly replicates this rejection of religious fanaticism for romantic love, and the moment in which Jane breaks from Rivers uses the same dramatic device. The May moon is shining. Rivers is inexorably pressing his demands. Jane is "tempted" to yield. She seems ready for the sacrifice. "The dim room was full of visions." She tells us, "I was excited more than I had ever been." Then, like the woman in "Apostasy" she hears, somehow, a distant voice crying her name, and she knows it's the voice of Rochester speaking "in pain and woe wildly, eerily, urgently." In this dramatic instance of the "Sympathies" in which Jane, and Brontë, believed, the voice of the man she loves interrupts her at the moment when she is in danger of a final, binding decision that would have separated them permanently. She finds the strength to defy Rivers. Jane is sure: this "is the work of nature. She was roused, and did—no miracle—but her best."

And so Jane Eyre must flee the happiness she had found at Moor House, abandoning the sisterly community of Diana, Mary, and Hannah, impelled by her need to soothe the pain and woe of the man she loves. In a curious paradox, like Rivers, and like the missionary in the poem of that name, she must reject what has turned out to be the lure of domestic happiness, which is not to be hers, and set out on the final stage of her journey—not toward some kind of specious glory, but instead toward compassion and love.

An Independent Woman

Writing to William S. Williams, the literary adviser to Smith, Elder early in 1848, Charlotte Brontë returned to the debate about realism and truth to experience versus the beguiling attractions of imagination and fantasy. She roundly asserted that in writing fiction she will never pretend to describe any "feeling, on any subject, public or private," of which she doesn't have real "experience." As we now examine the sequence of scenes that close *Jane Eyre,* it's again important to ask how Brontë was able to make such a claim. How, drawing upon her past, was she able to write about Jane's return to Thornfield, her shocked discovery of the building's ruin, of Rochester's injuries, and her reconciliation with him in the remote country house called Ferndean? Again, in uncanny ways, Brontë proves able to transform her experience, some of it thick with emotion and significance she hid, into the lithe and dramatic elements of the novel's happy ending. An ending that, at least at first glance, it would seem she had never enjoyed.

Breaking free from St. John Rivers' demands, Jane resolves to test the validity of her strange "inward sensation," a shock of feeling like an "earthquake." It seemed to be a kind of "privilege"—Brontë uses this term twice on the same page—that has liberated her spirit, and it has given her the opportunity for "free action." Much like a moment of religious conversion, it marks the real beginning of Jane as an independent woman. Demonstrating a self-confidence and resolve, and after a quick conversation with her cousins Diana and Mary in which she not so much requests their approval as simply announces what she is about to do, Jane packs her trunk and sets out by herself for the trip by coach back to Thornfield.

In many ways, Jane's decision to find Mr. Rochester repeats Brontë's determination to return, by herself, to Brussels in January 1843—a trip that was a willful effort to rejoin Constantin Heger. In both cases, the young woman takes considerable risks, defying propriety as she asserts her own judgment.

When Charlotte first traveled to Brussels, in February of 1842, she was accompanied, as was then proper, by her father and Emily. Indeed two family friends Mary and Joe Taylor went with them as far as London to help them with travel plans. And when Patrick and his two daughters arrived in Brussels, they were met by the Episcopal clergyman Mr. Jenkins and his wife, who took them to meet the Hegers at the pensionnat on the rue d'Isabelle. Throughout the journey Charlotte was overseen, protected, and governed by others, specifically by older men.

By contrast, when Charlotte returned to Brussels after the funeral for her aunt Branwell, she traveled alone. She had inherited a small sum of money on her aunt's death and may have used some of it to pay for her trip. This modest financial independence, somewhat amplified in the novel, permits Jane to pursue her married man. In Charlotte's case she was allowed to do so without any reservations— so far as we know—being expressed by her family. What Charlotte was doing was, like Jane Eyre, unusual for her era in terms of proper female conduct and was, in addition, physically demanding and risky. Charlotte in January of 1843 took the 9:00 AM railroad from Leeds to London arriving at 10:00 PM. Immediately, she got a cab that took her to London Bridge Wharf. There, the cabbie summarily took his money and left, while some watermen quarreled over Charlotte's trunk. Out on the water floating on a row boat near the Ostend packet there was a breathless moment when the deck crew refused permission to let her on the ship. Only through plucky self-confidence was she able to persuade one of them to let her board in the middle of the night. The packet sailed early the next morning and arrived in Ostend at 9:00 PM. Brontë stayed in a hotel overnight, on the next morning taking a train for Brussels arriving at 7:00 PM.

Jane Eyre tells the reader her trip to Thornfield took "six-and-thirty hours"—within an hour or so of the travel time—not counting her overnight in the hotel—of Charlotte's solitary trip to Brussels. She knew, very well, what she was writing about, and indeed created for Jane an easier and safer journey. In this we have yet another example of Brontë not telling the reader a worse, a darker truth.

The deeply—and secretly—autobiographical parallels between these paired journeys continues as Jane Eyre arrives, her heart leaping at the thought that she is "already on my master's very lands." Certainly Brontë felt just the same as she approached the school where over the past year she had gone through such powerful feelings of passion and dismay. When Jane's conscience tells her that because of his "lunatic wife" she fears that she has no possible future with Mr. Rochester, and that she should not speak to him, or see him, we can see the recklessness and indifference to the dangers and improprieties of her conduct that Brontë felt as she returned to encounter Heger after the passing of several months, now without her sister Emily. As Jane rushes through the woods eager to reach Thornfield in the early hours of the day, she voices the feelings that Charlotte must have experienced on the day of her return: "Who would be hurt by my once more tasting the life his glance can give me?" Who indeed, if not his wife.

At this point the close parallels between the two desperate journeys break. Charlotte found herself welcomed by Heger's wife. She returned to life as a teacher in the pensionnat. Jane finds something altogether darker yet more satisfying: Thornfield is a "blackened ruin," and Bertha has killed herself.

⬥

The fiery destruction of Mr. Rochester's family estate is clearly revenge: the fulfillment of the Creole Bertha Mason's frustrated erotic sensuality. Her efforts first to burn Rochester in his bed, and later to burn Jane's now empty bed, leads to the destruction of the entire building, making real the novel's concept of self-destructive Caribbean animal rage. The innkeeper who witnessed the scene remembers her as a "big woman," with long black hair "streaming against the flames." Brontë's image makes vividly real the mythical, punitive fury bestriding the inferno of her own making. And, as we discussed in Chapter Eight, she is at the same time a cautionary warning to Brontë to beware of an inclination to become her own fury.

There is in this moment a further curious and suggestive link to Brontë, and it causes us to return to our earlier discussion in Chapter Six of how she uses aspects of her father in the creation of her novel. There we considered Patrick's sometimes scarcely governable anger. Now we need to consider the influence of this complex man on Charlotte's imagination in two different and significantly related ways.

Ellen Nussey on her first visit to Haworth noticed that, unusually, the family home had no curtains and only two carpets—most of the floors being sanded stone—and learned this was the consequence of "Mr. Brontë's horror of fire." The same "dread" was, as she wrote, "so intense" that he would permit his daughters to wear dresses only made of silk or wool. Juliet Barker notes that his anxiety was based upon fact: "the high number of fatalities" in the town of Haworth caused by burning in domestic accidents, and Patrick had written to local newspapers warning people of this danger. Growing up in the Brontë household, Charlotte witnessed and learned to feel this dread and would readily have linked it to her father's fiery temper. As a novelist, she would have instinctively seized upon this interconnection between emotion and destruction.

One of Patrick's most powerful writings takes our exploration further. It deals with an event which took place on September 2, 1824. Swollen by heavy rain, two large areas of bog water, dammed up high in the moor land, burst open sending a seven foot wave of muddy water and peat sweeping down into the valley, tearing away stone bridges, overrunning fields and houses, and so polluting the local streams that the factories, which used their waters, were unable to operate for days. Patrick witnessed the oncoming thunderstorm, the heavens "blackening fast," the "frequent flashing of the light-

ning," and then heard "a deep, distant explosion" of the dams breaking and felt the parsonage itself trembling. Emily, Branwell, and
Anne were out for a walk with the servant Sara Garrs at that very
moment. The disaster, and the fact that his "little children" were
unhurt, seemed to him "a solemn visitation of Providence." An esti-
mated ten thousand people came to the area during the subsequent
days to witness the devastation. Patrick Brontë's response to this
event was to write both a poem, which he titled "The Phenomenon,"
and a prose sermon, in which he describes and then construes the
meaning of this—for the moment—celebrated event. He published
both at his own expense.

His poem begins as idyllic pastoral evoking evening bird song,
the milk-maid and "sturdy swain" laughing with "rural joy." In the
distance however he sees a "red portentious halo" in the sky, and it
causes him to consider that this scene, which seems to be like Eden,
is actually deceptive. Humanity has been driven out of Paradise by
"the flaming sword" of divine expulsion, and the poison from the
forbidden fruit has led to "passions fell and fierce" making all
humanity worthy of divine wrath, the "ire / Of justice imminent"
threatening "quenchless fire." Already we can see the parallels with
the burning of Thornfield emerging. Patrick is consciously writing
in the tradition of the prophet as visionary witness to the divine
meaning found in earthly disasters. His poetic/theological preface
leads to the kind of melodramatic nature writing that was so entic-
ing to Charlotte and Branwell. The night before the bog burst,
"reeling stars" shoot down "with slanting light," and a "crackling
blaze" hisses in the woods. A "bright halo" surrounds each cottage
candle. Now, on the evening of the disaster, birds wheel in the sky,
the sun sets in an ominous haze, a tempest with its whirlwinds and
"frequent lightning red" bursts overhead, the once-solid ground

suddenly begins to roll as if it were the ocean, and from the "riven mountain" erupts the flood. People flee, and it is only God who prevents further, overwhelming destruction. He draws the parallels with the world inundation at the time of Noah and the Ark, and he concludes by warning that the Christian vision of the end of the world will soon become real and then graceless souls will feel "a hell of dread" as "in the latest day of God's hot ire, / The earth and heavens will sink in liquid fire."

From her childhood Charlotte would have known this book, containing both the poem and the sermon to follow. Her father had intentionally written for young readers. The blackness of "that thick flood, that darkens, foams, and raves" becomes the terrifying blackness, the raving madness of Bertha's midnight apparitions. The lightning and the burning woods in the poem connect with the archetypal divine punishment—the flaming sword of the expelling angel, the "liquid fire" of the world's end—and become, in Charlotte's imagination, Bertha amidst the flames punishing and destroying the sexually passionate Mr. Rochester. The striking coincidence of the rhyme that Patrick uses twice in the poem: "ire / quenchless fire," and "God's hot ire / liquid fire," almost certainly lingered in Charlotte's mind, sparking this remarkable series of interconnections: Patrick's own rage, his vision of divine anger, and Bertha's "fierce" fulfillment as the exterminating angel of Thornfield executing vindictive punishment on the once-savage Mr. Rochester, now "blind and a cripple." All this ire is seething in Jane, and in Charlotte imagining Jane in this apocalyptic moment.

Thornfield is now nothing but a "blackened ruin." The same helpful innkeeper tells Jane that Mr. Rochester now lives in a remote house,

Ferndean. Like all the place names in Brontë's novel, this has meaning. "Dean," a word used frequently in the north of England and in
Scotland, comes from the Anglo-Saxon term for the valley of death,
and became used for the deep, narrow, wooded valley of a small
rivulet. Ferns, which have neither flowers nor seeds, reproduce by
spores, and spread freely in light-deprived, damp environments,
constituting some of the oldest surviving forms of plant life. Brontë
wants all of these suggestive associations with darkness and death.
Jane, ever impetuous, walks the last mile toward the house along a
grass-grown track gloomy, damp, flowerless, and overarched by
"close-ranked" trees. In the dim twilight she can barely make out
the "deep buried" building, "so dank and green were its decaying
walls." She wonders if there can be any life in a place such as this. It
seems a place where there is "no opening anywhere." Indeed, Mr.
Rochester seems buried alive, an eerie fulfillment of Brontë's earlier
fascination, discussed in Chapter Two, with this grim fate.

As Jane Eyre halts at the edge of the woods a figure emerges from
the house. At once she recognizes him: "my master." At this moment
Edward Fairfax Rochester still has the traits Brontë has derived from
the important men in her secret life. His "erect port," his "raven-black"
hair, her idealized recollection of Contstantin Heger, are still there; his
"athletic strength" and "vigorous prime" derived from Zamorna
remain. But there has been a change. He seems now like a "wronged
and fettered beast," much like her shattered Branwell, trammeled now
by self-pity and self-destructive addiction to the point where he
describes himself as "a thoroughly *old man*—mentally and bodily."
He has become exactly like Charlotte's fictional Henry Hastings, a
man who has "wasted his vigour and his youth in vice," still though
with a "dark, fiery eye," but now under a brow marked with "the various lines of suffering, passion and profligacy." In Rochester's blindness

now "all to him" Jane guesses, "was void darkness," exactly the condition in which her father found himself as he first began to recover from his eye operation during those same months, fretting and festering at his inability to return to his clerical duties, an invalid stuck in the Haworth parsonage.

⁂

Charlotte has Jane refuse to accept Rochester's condition. While with mounting anger Charlotte found that her brother ignored all efforts to help him, her father Patrick was ready to be cared for and longed to get better. So when Jane tells Rochester that she is not the result of his own "sweet madness," but a real woman, an "independent woman," he accepts her willingness to be "a kind little nurse," for whom he should entertain, as he remarks with bitter frustration, a "fatherly feeling."

While Charlotte had to make do with her father's thanks for her help, Jane will gain a happiness Charlotte did not experience. Rochester tells Jane of the terrible months after her flight from Thornfield. He remembers now the "hot tears" he "wept over our separation." As she writes these lines Brontë may recall her own years since her forced separation from Heger. Still she and Jane can utter the same pledge: "All my heart is yours, sir, it belongs to you; and with you it would remain were fate to exile the rest of me from your presence forever." In Brontë's case, fate has dictated exactly this exile, and no one sees, or cares, for her extraordinary fidelity. She knows what love in exile feels like. She knows its empty bitterness. Brontë's assertion that the authenticity of the novel stems from her having experienced such moments rings true, even if she suffers only loss where Jane ultimately finds joy.

As Rochester recovers partial eyesight he becomes more like

Charlotte's father. Groping, dutiful, submissive. Rochester's happiness at Jane's willingness to marry leads him to prayerful gratitude and the rhetoric Charlotte knew well from her father: "my heart swells with gratitude to the beneficent God of this earth." In confessing that he once had treated her wrongly, Rochester begins to speak in the very same terms we find in Patrick's "The Phenomenon." Patrick intones that the wise man should be "thankful" that he is spared, and should "Despise not this merciful, but monitory voice of Divine Wisdom." The good man must hear, and "learn to be spiritually wise," lest the day come suddenly "when God 'Will laugh at your calamity . . . when . . . your destruction commeth as a whirlwind; when distress and anguish cometh upon you.'" Now Rochester interprets for Jane their past in similar terms: "Divine justice pursued its course; disasters came thick on me . . . *His* chastisements are mighty . . . only of late—I began to see and acknowledge the hand of God in my doom. I began to experience remorse . . . the wish for reconcilement to my Maker."

Thus, in a peculiarly ironic return, Brontë has come to imagine Jane Eyre's happiness in terms of the restricted life that family obligations have imposed on her. The Haworth parsonage, haunted by death and self-destruction, is nevertheless the home where she can restore her beloved father to a vital and effective life. Rochester, now very like Patrick, loves and depends on her. Never very interested in children, Brontë has Jane pass over with remarkable brevity Adèle's transformation into a "pleasing" companion, "docile, good-tempered, and well-principled." Jane's son gets but a single sentence. While the sisterhood of Moor House is no longer hers, Diana and Mary, now married, visit Ferndean alternate years. Ellen Nussey shared similar visits with Charlotte, though both remain unmarried.

Charlotte's novel concludes in the same complex autobiographical manner that it began. If its depiction of happiness is not radiantly liberating, neither was her life. Brontë as author and as woman seems to have, for the moment, followed her father's instruction and become "spiritually wise."

Epilogue

Charlotte Brontë received her first six printed copies of *Jane Eyre* on October 19, 1847. Early reviews, as we have seen, were very positive, and the book soon was a best seller, going into second and third editions within months. Early in 1848 she told her father Patrick of her success. In July she went to London to tell her publishers at Smith, Elder that she was "Currer Bell." This tiny circle remained, for some time, the only people who knew the identity of the novel's author.

Now, tragedy descended on the Brontës. Two-and-a-half months later, on September 24, Branwell died, almost certainly of tuberculosis. Soon thereafter Emily's health began to fail from the same cause, and, sternly refusing medical aid until her last hours, she died on December 19. Both were buried in the family vault in the Haworth church, their names inscribed on the wall plaque along with those of their mother and older sisters. Charlotte and her friend Ellen Nussey took Anne, who was already showing symptoms of tuberculosis, to the seaside town of Scarborough, where she died a half-year later on May 28, 1849. Charlotte had her buried there. Grief almost overwhelmed her. On June 25 she wrote to Williams, "waking – I think – sleeping – I dream of them." And this haunting was not the worst of it. She continues, "I cannot recall them as they were in health – still they appear to me in sickness and suffering."

In the end she did not give in. Instead, difficult though it was for her, she carried on with the writing of her third novel. Incredible as it seems, the book was published just a few months after Anne's death on October 26 with a title page reading: *SHIRLEY. / A Tale.* / By / CURRER BELL, / AUTHOR OF "JANE EYRE". Though Emily's earlier demands that the Brontës publish under pseudonyms meant little now that her younger sisters were dead, Charlotte continued to insist upon one. Writing to Elizabeth Gaskell on November 17, who at the time knew that "Currer Bell" was a woman but nothing more, Brontë argued her chief reason for maintaining the pseudonym was the "fear that if she relinquished it, strength and courage would leave her, and she would ever after shrink—from writing the plain truth." So there it is again, the insistence on fact. And, indeed, in *Shirley,* just as with *Jane Eyre,* Brontë created characters and situations immediately drawn from her experience, even though she set this novel early in the nineteenth century. Some of her characters' sources were so clear that the victims of her satirical portraits of a group of local curates immediately recognized themselves, but, as she wrote Williams, rather than expressing indignation "each characteristically finds solace for his own wounds in crowing over his brethren." The practice of secret history was thus continuing.

However, as the months passed, more and more people heard about or guessed that Charlotte Brontë was Currer Bell. Finally, on

February 28, 1850, the *Bradford Observer* published a gossipy note: "It is understood that the only daughter of the Rev P Brontë, incumbent of Haworth is the authoress of *Jane Eyre* and *Shirley*," adding that both books had appeared "under the name of 'Currer Bell.'"

By this time many of Charlotte's immediate acquaintances knew that, unlikely as it might seem, this tiny and often reclusive woman from a small town in Yorkshire had written two major novels. She became sought after during her ever more frequent trips to London. Friends took her to the opera, to the Great Exhibition of 1851, to museums, even gaining an entry to the woman's gallery to hear a debate in Parliament.

This life of seeming celebrity and pleasure did not make her happy. She confessed to Ellen Nussey on August 25, 1852, "my life is a pale blank and often a very weary burden." Rather than relishing an optimism based on her success, "the Future sometimes appalls me." The reason, she asserted almost angrily, was "not that I am a single woman and likely to remain a single woman—but because I am a lonely woman and likely to be lonely."

Still, she persisted in writing. By October 26, 1852, as she was nearing the completion of her fourth novel she—quite incredibly—wrote her editor Williams, "My wish is that the book should be published without Author's name." Two days later she further explained to George Smith, the publisher and by this time a good friend of hers, "I should be most thankful for the sheltering shadow of an incognito. I seem to dread the advertisements." Of course Smith, Elder could not agree. To publish anonymously would be to almost certainly eliminate any hope for successful sales. In the end the book finally appeared on January 28, 1853, as "VILLETTE. / BY CURRER BELL, / AUTHOR OF 'JANE EYRE,' 'SHIRLEY,' ETC."

Charlotte's anxiety about the "truth" behind this book and her futile wish to hide behind the old pseudonym were well founded. All the central characters came from her life, indeed, from the most intensely emotional moments of that life. Again the reader is taken to Brussels, the scene of the earlier novel *The Professor*. Its central male character, Paul Emanuel, is modeled on Constantin Heger, while his wife Mme. Beck is based upon Mme. Zoe Heger. The book's heroine Lucy Snowe is a thinly veiled portrait of Charlotte, her moods and depression drawn from Brontë's during the months she was writing the novel. Doctor John Bretton closely resembles the handsome publisher George Smith, and Lucy's feelings for him suggest that Charlotte was inclined to fall in love with Smith, a relationship which was never to be, Smith marrying another in 1854. So transparently autobiographical was *Villette* for the people portrayed, that when Mme. Heger came upon a pirated French version published in 1855, she immediately recognized herself, her husband, and the complex and dangerous emotions that had driven their former English pupil. When Elizabeth Gaskell arrived in late spring of 1856 to make inquiries as she researched her biography of Brontë, Mme. Heger refused to see her.

Then, finally, the solution to Brontë's loneliness unexpectedly appeared. Arthur Bell Nicholls had been Patrick Brontë's curate since June of 1845, a raw young man from the north of Ireland. Charlotte's early assessment to Ellen was the "narrowness of his mind always strikes me chiefly." As time passed she largely ignored him, caught up in the excitement of her success as a writer and then the sudden tragedies she suffered as a sister. And so, in December of 1852, with the manuscript of *Villette* just sent to London, he astonished her by seeking to talk with her privately one evening in the

Haworth rectory, speaking emotionally of the "sufferings" he had endured for a long time as he found himself drawn into loving her. Putting him off for the moment, Charlotte informed her father. Patrick responded in a rage: "Papa worked himself into a state not to be trifled with—the veins on his temples started up like whip-cord—and his eyes became suddenly blood-shot."

Brontë's father had two principal reasons for his angry rejection of this proposal. The first was that it seemed to him his junior assistant was working behind his back and without his agreement. The second was that Nicholls was in every way inferior to his daughter. As she put it to Ellen, he told her "the match would be a degradation—that I should be throwing myself away." Charlotte refused him. Nicholls continued in his clerical duties, treated with icy silence by her father. Charlotte found herself feeling that "silent pity is just all I can give him." As time passed and she felt more and more sympathy for the man—and perhaps defiance at her father's effort to control her life—she confessed to Ellen that she had begun to fear that she might lose "the purest gem . . . the most precious - life can give – genuine attachment." Meanwhile Nicholls agreed to leave for another posting. Just before his departure Charlotte met him, "leaning against the garden-door in a paroxysm of anguish - sobbing as women never sob." Though exiled, Nicholls nevertheless corresponded with her. While he was visiting some friends in the neighborhood early in 1854, they would meet on a country lane to talk together. By February Patrick acceded to Charlotte's demands, and Nicholls began to visit the Haworth parsonage again. On June 29, 1854, they were married.

What ensued was perhaps the happiest time in Brontë's life. The married couple traveled to Ireland to meet Nicholls' family. There, friends and servants told Charlotte, "I have got one of the best gentlemen in the country." She was impressed by the splendid home of his uncle where Arthur had been raised. They continued to the west of Ireland where Charlotte was struck by its wild beauty. She was spellbound when on cliffs overlooking the Atlantic she watched the waves sweep to the shore, and she told her new husband she wished to stay there for a while. Silently taking in the scene, he covered her up with a rug "to keep off the spray," only holding her back when she went "near the edge of the cliff." Later Charlotte wrote to Ellen of "the kind and ceaseless protection which has ever surrounded me," as Nicholls assiduously cared for her well-being.

Back home at Haworth, the married couple, now living in the parsonage together, Nicholls became caught up again in his daily duties. Charlotte found her life very changed. He needed her help, and she found that "to be wanted continually, to be constantly called for and occupied seems so strange; yet it is a marvelously good thing." In her letters, the woman who had for so many decades imagined and longed for the love of "my Master," now writes joyfully of "my dear boy."

Then, with cruel swiftness, there came a change. On January 19 Charlotte writes to Ellen that for ten days, that is, since January 9, she has had stomach problems and is sometimes faint. "I certainly never before felt as I have done lately." On January 30, a local doctor confirms she is pregnant. By February 14 Nicholls is writing to Ellen that Charlotte is "completely prostrated with weakness and sickness and frequent fever." At about the same time, Charlotte wrote to her friend Amelia Taylor, who had recently given birth, about her condition: "Sickness with scarce a reprieve—I strain until what I vomit is mixed with blood." She wrote another friend about Nicholls, "No kinder, better husband than mine, it seems to me, there can be in the world. I do not want now for kind companionship in health and the tenderest nursing in sickness." And so she wasted away, becoming skeletally thin, her hands seemingly transparent. She could no longer hold a pencil. She died on March 31, 1855. Her father quietly, and perhaps bitterly, remarked to a servant, "I always told you Martha, that there was no sense in Charlotte marrying at all, for she was not strong enough for marriage."

For six years Nicholls remained at Haworth carrying on with the ill-paid, subsidiary job of curate, aiding the aging Patrick in his clerical duties. On his death in June of 1861, Charlotte's father left his entire estate, as had she, to the Rev. Nicholls. He returned to Banagher in the north of Ireland taking Charlotte's "dresses and manuscripts and drawings—which," as Winifred Gèrin notes, "he refused to regard as anything but tender keepsakes concerning none but himself." Nicholls married a second time, to a cousin, and lived until December 3, 1906.

For most of her life Charlotte Brontë lived two lives. She was the docile, hardworking, and disciplined child of a Yorkshire clergyman following the rules and practices of her time and place. At the same time she lived an extravagant, rebellious, sensuous, and powerfully emotional life in her imagination. This she projected first through the voluminous unpublished writing of her early years. Later, through her four published novels, she invented that complex interplay of the "truthful" record of observation and experience merged with the bright projections of her dreams and her longings that became the mark of her genius.

Everything about the external physical appearance of Charlotte Brontë—the stunted growth, the pale skin, the bad teeth—can be at least partially accounted for by the strains of her past, even as her tiny body and plain face won her sympathy and lifelong friends. While it had been in one way a very painful, strange, and damaged life, in another it had been frequently blissfully happy and nurturing. The novels record these disparities that gave her the character, like her heroines, to succeed in pursuing her own way.

Charlotte's reserve, her clear, penetrating gaze, her aloof demeanor, as well as her sharp-tongue, were a part of a thorny defense mechanism she had created to deal with the inferiority of the roles she was forced to play, which she indignantly knew to be unfair, and which she abandoned as quickly as she could.

Secrecy, an "'Ostrich-longing for concealment' as she called it," had indeed been an important theme even in her earlier, unpublished writing. Her heroine Elizabeth Hastings in many ways, as we have seen, much like Brontë herself, seemed "an insignificant, unattractive young woman" though she secretly concealed "intense emotions . . . always smothered under diffidence and prudence and a skillful address." In that dynamic we find both the truth of the drab realism of daily life as lived by a young, mid-Victorian woman and the powerful inner life bred by imagination and making claim to an equal kind of truth, the truth of inner experience felt as violent, painful, and in itself real.

Charlotte, on the first page of her 1846 novel *The Professor*, wrote of "what stores of romance and sensibility lie hidden in breasts" that no one suspects to be "casketing such treasures." In a poem probably from that same year she uses the same key term:

> The human heart has hidden treasures,
> In secret kept, in silence sealed;—
> The thoughts, the hopes, the dreams, the pleasures,
> Whose charms were broken if revealed.

The paradox is that as a writer she revealed those hidden treasures of thought, hope, dream, and pleasure, but sought to protect herself from the damage of public scrutiny by concealing the autobiographical roots through the strategies of fiction. As these pages show, *Jane Eyre* is "An Autobiography." A liberation of Brontë's inner life—and much of her lived experience—recounted according to the "dictation" of an eloquent and urgent imagination.

When the well-known critic Harriet Martineau visited the family home in Haworth in later years, after the death of Charlotte's brother and two sisters, at a time when the novelist was living alone with Patrick, she felt "something inexpressibly affecting in the aspect of the frail little creature who had done such wonderful things, and who was able to bear up, with so bright an eye and so composed a countenance, under not only such a weight of sorrow, but such a prospect of solitude. In her deep mourning dress (neat as a Quaker's), with her beautiful hair, smooth and brown, her fine eyes, and her sensible face indicating a habit of self-control, she seemed a perfect household image." Reading *Jane Eyre* we know how much of a personal victory Brontë had achieved through that self-control and how many secrets her composed countenance had concealed.

Acknowledgments

Lauren Clark of Kuhn Projects initially suggested that I investigate "how" Charlotte Brontë wrote *Jane Eyre,* and I am indebted to her for her faith and hard work in making the project real. Amy Cherry and her colleague Remy Cawley at W. W. Norton believed in this book and worked tirelessly to improve it.

Everyone studying the life and work of Charlotte Brontë is indebted to the scholarship and wisdom of Elizabeth Gaskell, Winifrith Gérin, Juliet Barker, and Claire Harmon for their biographies of this complex woman. Thanks to the incredible industry of Christine Alexander, Victor A. Neufeldt, and Heather Glen we now have reliable texts of the Brontë juvenilia. And everyone working the field is indebted to Margaret Smith for her magisterial edition of the letters.

I'm very grateful for the help in researching this book of two generous Georgetown students, Marielle Hampe and Emily Coccia. Carole Sargent offered important publishing advice, and from the Lauinger Library Melissa Jones and Meg Oakley offered invaluable insight and assistance. Karen Lautman gave invaluable help in arranging for needed funding. Many colleagues in the Georgetown English Department offered generous encouragement.

My dear wife Sissy Seiwald carried me through the years of work on this book with patience and love, and it makes me very happy to be able to dedicate it to her.

Notes

THE TEXT OF *JANE EYRE*

Quotations from Charlotte Brontë's *Jane Eyre* come from Richard J. Dunn's edition of the novel (W. W. Norton: New York, 2001), and page numbers are cited in the endnotes by a key phrase taken *from the beginning of the paragraph* in question as JE and the page number.

This volume is also the source for further texts, such as selections from Brontë's "Roe Head Journal," which are cited in key-phrase endnotes as JE and the page number.

ENDNOTES

Other endnotes for each chapter using key phrases *from later in a given paragraph* cite sources and provide further information.

Endnotes referring to a second citation for a source *infrequently used* cite its author and a page reference. For example, "Johnson 149."

Endnotes for all correspondence cite the writer of the letter and then its recipient using abbreviations for names. Hence a letter from Charlotte Brontë to Ellen Nussey is cited as, for example, CB to EN Letters I, 184.

Abbreviations: Correspondents

CB	Charlotte Brontë
BB	Branwell Brontë
CH	Constantin Heger
EB	Emily Brontë
EG	Elizabeth Gaskell

EN	Ellen Nussey
GS	George Smith
HC	Hartley Coleridge
HN	Henry Nussey
MW	Margaret Wooler
RS	Robert Southey
WSW	William Smith Wilson

Abbreviations: Frequently Used Sources

AB AG	Anne Brontë, *Agnes Grey* (Oxford: Oxford University Press, 2010).
Allott	Miriam Allott, *The Brontës. The Critical Heritage* (London: Routledge, 1974).
CA EW	Christine Alexander ed., *An Edition of the Early Writings of Charlotte Brontë* (Oxford: Oxford University Press, 1987, 1992).
CA SW	Christine Alexander ed., *The Brontës: Tales of Glass Town, Angria, and Gondal. Selected Writings* (Oxford: Oxford University Press, 2010).
Catalogue	Christine Alexander and Jane Sellars, *The Art of the Brontës* (Cambridge: Cambridge University Press, 1995).
CB *High Life*	Charlotte Brontë, *High Life in Verdopolis*, ed. Christine Alexander (London: British Library, 1995).
CB TP	Charlotte Brontë, *The Professor* (Oxford: Oxford University Press, 2008).
CH	Clare Harman, *Charlotte Brontë: A Fiery Heart* (New York: Knopf, 2016).
Chitham	Edward Chitham, *A Brontë Family Chronology* (Houndmills: Palgrave Macmillan, 2003).
EG	Elizabeth Gaskell, *The Life of Charlotte Brontë*, ed. Angus Easson (Oxford: Oxford University Press, 2001).
HG	Heather Glen, ed., *Charlotte Brontë Tales of Angria* (London: Penguin, 2006).
JB	Julia Barker, *The Brontës* (New York: Pegasus, 2013).
JE	Charlotte Brontë, *Jane Eyre. Norton Critical Edition*, ed. Richard J. Dunn (New York: W. W. Norton, 2001).
Letters	Margaret Smith, ed., *The Letters of Charlotte Brontë with a Selection of Letters by Family and Friends, Volume I: 1829–1847* (Oxford: Oxford University Press, 1995), *Volume II: 1848–1851* (Oxford: Oxford University Press, 2000), *Volume III: 1852–1855* (Oxford: Oxford University Press, 2004).
Lonoff	Sue Lonoff, ed., *The Belgian Essays* (New Haven, CT: Yale University Press, 1996).

N CBP   Victor A. Neufeldt, *The Poems of Charlotte Brontë, A New Text and Commentary* (New York: Garland, 1985).

N PPBB   Victor A. Neufeldt, *The Poems of Patrick Branwell Brontë* (New York: Garland, 1990).

N WPBB   Victor A. Neufeldt, *The Works of Patrick Branwell Brontë Volume I* (New York: Garland, 1997), Volume II (New York: Garland, 1999).

Orel   Harold Orel, The Brontës. Interviews and Recollections (Iowa City: University of Iowa Press, 1997).

Ox Comp   Christine Alexander and Margaret Smith, The Oxford *Companion to the Brontës* (Oxford: Oxford University Press, 2003).

Poems 1846   Charlotte, Emily, and Anne Brontë, *Poems by Currer, Ellis and Acton Bell* (Hannah Wilson, 2015).

WG   Winifred Gérin, *Charlotte Brontë: The Evolution of Genius* (Oxford: Oxford University Press, 1968).

INTRODUCTION

11   **"Eyes with tears."** Allott, 69, 67–68.

12   **"Under cover to Miss Brontë."** CB to Smith, Elder and Co., Letters I, 533.

13   **Far more complicated.** Dated by her 19 September 1850, published 7 December 1850 Chitham 214; Orel 133ff. See also Emily Brontë, *Wuthering Heights*, ed. Richard J. Dunn (New York: W. W. Norton, 2003), 307, 312.

13   **"Into a fortress."** JB 797; Orel 99.

15   **Twenty-first-century.** CB to CH, Letters I, 379–80.

CHAPTER ONE

22   **Become *Jane Eyre*.** CB to CH, Letters I, 379.

22   **As we shall see.** JE 378.

23   **Risk-taking heroine.** CB to WSW, Letters I, 546.

25   **Their own rights.** JE 444–45. A friend of many distinguished Victorian writers and intellectuals and a novelist in his own right, Lewes was to begin living with the writer Mary Ann Evans in 1854 and encouraged her to write fiction under the pseudonym George Eliot.

25   **It is thus a book.** JE 295, emphasis added.

26   **Intensity was always there.** HG 258.

27   **A "very limited" life.** JE 26.

27   **There are other.** JE 298, 316.

03   **She had sought.** See Tom Winnifrith, *The Brontës and Their Back-ground: Romance and Reality* (New York: Barnes and Noble, 1973), 75. EG 247.

31   **"Sin and Suffering . . ."** See Charlotte Brontë, *Jane Eyre*, eds. Jane Jack and Margaret Smith (Oxford: Oxford University Press, 1969), xi–xii. CB to EN, Letters I, 497.

31   **More real than life.** Allott 303–4. EG 245–46.

32   **"May be already defective."** In rejecting Charlotte's earlier novel *The Professor* the editors at Smith, Elder had expressed an interest in seeing another novel, and she promised them this would be "of a more strik-ing and exciting character." CB to Smith, Elder and Co., Letters I, 535, 539.

CHAPTER TWO

33   **"Ten times a day."** WG 327. CB to EN, Letters I, 492. EG 245. WG 328. CB to EN, Letters I, 500.

34   **Curt note of rejection.** CB to EN, Letters I, 493, 498.

34   **"There was no possibility of taking a walk that day."** JE 5.

34   **Jane goes on.** JE 12, 19. CB to EN, Letters I, 284.

35   **As the story begins.** JE 5–6.

36   **"The Roe Head Journal."** JE 404–5.

36   **Private and secret reveries.** JE 399.

37   **Her sexual longing.** JE 422.

37   **Inappropriate for a young woman.** CB to EN, Letters I, 144.

37   **This book is crucial.** JE 216.

37   **What is happening to her.** "By the time she wrote *Jane Eyre*, Charlotte was convinced of the importance of the pictorial image in stimulating the creative process. Jane's experience confirms the way pictures tell a story, not always of the physical world but of the psychological. There is no moment where she is aware of a conceptual leap from copying to imaginative painting, but her author uses this significant creative advance to indicate Jane's inner reality." Christine Alexander, "Edu-cating 'The Artist's Eye': Charlotte Brontë and the Pictorial Image," in *The Brontës in the World of the Arts*, eds. Sandra Hagan and Juliette Wells (Aldershot: Ashgate, 2008), 28.

39   **Through the moors near death.** Dated 27 November 1832. N CBP 100, lines 9–12.

39   **"Lustre cold and bright."** N CBP, 101, lines 37–38, 45–48.

39   **Ancient isolated pillar.** N CBP 102, lines 75–76.

39   **And so when Charlotte.** JE 5, 6–7.

40 "Explained it very well." EG 82.

41 **Present in her description.** Thomas Bewick, *A History of British Birds, Volume II* (London: Bernard Quaritch, 1885), 185.

41 **As the list continues.** JE 6.

41 **Immanence of the diabolical.** Thomas Bewick, *A History of British Birds, Volume I* (London: Bernard Quaritch, 1885), 103, 232. This may have suggested to Emily Brontë the scene in which Isabella Linton discovers Heathcliff has hung her lap dog.

42 **Her personal haven.** JE 422, 400–1. Much later in the novel Rochester remembers secretly observing Jane lapsing into "a deep reverie" where she dreams a "day vision" that pleases her, only to be interrupted by Mrs. Fairfax "speaking to a servant in the hall . . ." JE 267. The pattern of this scene exactly replicates Charlotte's experience.

42 **It is John Reed.** JE 7, 8.

43 **Cutting her head.** CB TP 56. AB AG 20, 23, 27.

44 **Threw a Bible at her.** EG 136. JB 364.

44 **John Reed defiles.** JB 11.

44 **During the ensuing scuffle.** JE 9.

45 **Mrs. Reed arrives.** JE 23, 9.

45 **As Jane's rage dwindles.** JE 13.

46 **From earlier gothic fiction.** CB to EN, Letters I, 178. CB to MW, Letters I, 505.

47 **Horrifying as a nightmare.** CA EW 272. HG 456–7.

47 **Threatened with supernatural visitations.** EG 111.

48 **"All buried here."** Eighteen forty-two was a particularly devastating year. William Weightman, a handsome young curate whose dash and charm had endeared him to all, helped Patrick Brontë in the church. Charlotte had drawn an elegant portrait of him in 1840. On September 6, he was to die of cholera at age twenty-eight. Martha Taylor, sister to Charlotte's friend Mary—living in Brussels where Charlotte and Emily were studying—died of the same terrible malady on October 2 at age twenty-three. Martha was in many ways similar to Charlotte. In reacting to this loss, Charlotte wrote a poem describing Martha as a flower; but now, "The rose is blasted withered blighted / Its root has felt a worm." Finally the kindly Aunt Branwell, who had been a surrogate mother to the family for many years, died on October 29 at age sixty-six after suffering for days from a painful obstruction of the bowel. These three deaths were terrible blows to Charlotte and her siblings. Summing up the meaning of these losses in November she writes, "Aunt—Martha Taylor—Mr. Weightman are now all gone— how dreary & void everything seems." CB to EN, Letters I, 302. EG 99. HG 459. CB to EN, Letters I, 385.

48 Indeed the return of the vengeful dead. JE 10, 14.

49 Darkness of Jane's in the red-room. "Gilbert" in N CBP 401–4.

50 And then come consolations. JE 15, 16–17.

50 Indeed, Jane must leave. JE 35.

51 Each is a test. Frequently Jane is described as on a pilgrimage, critics discerning the influence of Bunyan's *Pilgrim's Progress* (1678) on Brontë's book. It is, however, illuminating to consider *Jane Eyre* as part of this larger and much older narrative tradition in which Bunyan's tale plays a small but significant part. The most thought-provoking discussion of this topic is Joseph Campbell's 1949 study, *The Hero with a Thousand Faces*, commemorative edition (Princeton, NJ: Princeton University Press, 2004).

CHAPTER THREE

52 Thus in framing. JE 49, 30.

53 Mrs. Reed wants. JE 27, 28, 29.

54 Truth about her own past. JB 158.

55 Triumph in her words. CB to Smith, Elder and Co., Letters I, 539–40. EG 51. CB to WSW, Letters II, 3–4.

56 Rely on them here. EG 60, 475.

56 Her sisters but also herself. EG 57.

57 Indifferent strangers. CB to HN, Letters I, 255.

58 What Brontë writes. JE 28.

58 When Jane arrives at Lowood. JE 36, 37.

60 Underlying the structure. JE 39.

61 Although it evokes much. Gérin discusses in ample detail how Wilson's Calvinism led to his conviction that eternal damnation punishes "the wicked, among whom must be classed the naughty child . . ." WG 12, 7.

61 For individuals. JE 38, 45, 47.

61 A punishment for all the girls. JE 38, 61.

62 Accumulated during the week. EG 476–77. WG 8. EG 56.

62 All is done. JE 41, 50.

63 Little which they have. WG 9.

63 Brontë depicts the inner spring. JE 54.

64 Certainly half freethinking. EG 478, 476. Letters II, 280, n. 5.

64 To show how close. JE 56–57.

65 Steels herself for the worst. Brontë, *Jane Eyre*, eds. Jack and Smith, figure facing 621.

65 When the span of time. JE 58.

65 Brontë remembers another sister. JE 40–41.

65   It is here Jane first meets. JE 41.

66   Dead sister, Maria. CA EW I, 256-57.

66   Lively and engaged fashion. Letters I, Appendix, 593. CB to WSW, Letters II, 279.

67   "Had been subjected." EG 41. CB to WSW, Letters I, 553. EG 57.

67   Punished for being late. WG 11. EG 58.

68   Her guilt because she is still alive. JB 162–63.

69   Reincarnate Maria. JE 414.

69   As Helen comforts Jane. JE 59.

69   Maria Temple greeted Jane. JE 60 -62.

70   Repress and cut off. JB 62. After the publication of *Jane Eyre*, her father "placed a packet of letters yellowed with age" into her hands one day saying, "These are your Mother's letters . . ." She and Ellen Nussey read them, moved by "Her gentleness and lovingness, her purity and refinement, her goodness and modesty." Letters I, Appendix, 608. Catalogue #36.

71   "The fever." EG 59.

71   Nine years old. Chitham, 42–43, lays out the problem as to when Charlotte and Emily returned from Cowan Bridge, either in early June or in late August. While being at home as Elizabeth died would have had a powerful impact on these young children, even if they returned after her death the tragedy lingered in their minds and hearts.

71   At eleven at night. JE 68, 69.

71   Helen's last words. JE 70.

72   The next morning Miss Temple. JE 70.

CHAPTER FOUR

73   Time moves quickly. JE 70.

74   This process of development. JE 32, 33.

74   The novel's readers already know. JE 8–9.

76   "Very strange ones." EG 69.

77   No question. JB 182–83. See note for pg. 71 in EG 481. EG 70. CA SW 498.

77   Sharing what they learned. JB 188, 193.

77   "An Adventure in Ireland." CA SW 15–17.

79   Jane remains at Lowood. JE 71.

79   After Helen's death. JE 71.

80   "A strong Irish accent." Letters I, Appendix, 589, 590. JB 200.

80   Her almost foreign accent. Letters I, Appendix, 591.

81   "interesting to me." WG 65.

81   **Charlotte's artistic ambition.** Catalogue 191 #62. Letters I, Appendix, 603.

81   **Jane Eyre, too, from her youthful days.** JE 63.

83   **Chapter XXIII of *Jane Eyre*.** JB 205. Letters I, Appendix, 596.

83   **Marginal position at Rochester's house parties.** JB 205–07.

84   **"Incorrigible 'Booby.'"** *Ox Comp*, 290. CB to EN, Letters I, 148.

84   **"Sensible pursuits their ennui."** CB to EN, Letters I, 511.

85   **Such an opportunity.** CB to EN, Letters I, 127.

85   **The human heart.** CB to EN, Letters I, 128.

86   **Own willed decision.** CB to EN, Letters I, 130.

86   **1825 to 1835 were thus happy.** JE 72.

CHAPTER FIVE

87   **The reproach.** JE 10.

87   **In seeking a new form.** JE 75.

87   **At Thornfield Hall.** Marielle Hampe in her recent MA thesis "To Grow Up Clean: Jane Eyre and Education" (Georgetown University, 2016) surveyed 150 such advertisements for work as governess published between 1790 and 1840 and has shown conclusively both that there was a commonly used format for these personal ads, which included specific set phrases such as "good English education," and that Brontë has given Jane's exactly that format. See page 20 and following for Hampe's extensive and detailed account.

88   **Current mental state.** RS to CB, Letters I, 166–67.

88   **Religiously sanctioned certitude.** RS to CB, Letters I, 166–67. Robert Southey (1774–1843) was named Laureate in 1813, a reward in part for his earlier shift from radical to political conservative. He is most remembered now for his biography of Lord Nelson (1813) and for Byron's savage attack on him as a turncoat and sycophant in "The Vision of Judgment" (1822).

89   **Unhappiness of Charlotte Brontë's daily life.** "I scarce would let that restless eye." N CBP 238–39.

89   **Jane Eyre presents.** JE 71.

90   **"Too excited or too despondent."** JB 490.

90   **"I believe that I have Genius."** JB 490. In order not to seem excessively boastful, Charlotte put this affirmation into the words of a letter from a fictional "Poor Painter" addressed to "a Great Lord." But to anyone knowing what Brontë was going through during the months when she wrote the piece it is impossible not to believe the poor painter stands in for herself. Lonoff 358, 360.

91   **Not so easy to achieve.** HG 452, 455.

92   Present in Mr. Rochester. N PCB 186–89.
92   Charlotte gives Jane. JE 72.
92   The liberty she desires. JB 490.
93   She had to flee. CH 64, 67. JB 335. CB to EN, Letters I, 178.
94   Before starting *Jane Eyre*. AB AG 12, 20, 28.
94   Years later Charlotte Brontë. JE 11.
95   That novel's first chapters. EG 135–36. CB to WSW, Letters II, 65.
96   "Love the *governess*, my dear!" JB 361. CB to EB, Letters I, 190–91. CB to EN, Letters I, 194. EG 136.
96   Employment in July. WG 147–48.
97   Curiously and significantly. JE 29.
98   "Very thoughts of governess-ship." EG 144.
98   Gratitude on both sides. Chitham 118 notes the exact date when she began cannot be determined. EG 158. CB to EN, Letters I, 246–47, 253. EG 164.
99   French to the end of the year. CB to EN, Letters I, 289.
99   "[Were] mentally depraved." CB TP 46–47, 81, 82.
100   A similarly flawed. JE 88, 87, 124, 74.
101   Before leaving for Thornfield. JE 75.
102   Primly and, frequently, alludes. CB to EB, Letters I, 191. CB to EN, Letters I, 248.
102   On this same first morning. JE 85.

CHAPTER SIX

103   Fairfax Rochester himself. JE 118.
104   What Charlotte Brontë. JE 97, 96.
105   Everything about the man. JE 98.
106   Newfoundland dog Pilot. Clearly an echo of Mr. Sidgwick's Newfoundland dog.
106   In Elizabeth Gaskell's biography. JE 123, 263.
107   Patrick Brontë's rage. EG 44, 471.
108   Her views on an issue. Letters I, Appendix, 599, 608. EG 471. WG 575. Letters I, Appendix, 607.
109   One aspect. JE 99.
111   Their shared lives. WG 20.
111   What began in play. JE 134.
111   Glimpsing their fencing. JB 224.
111   This kind of fun. Spelling and punctuation from original text. N WPBB I, 92.
112   Passed around the table. CA EW 1, 180–81.
113   Bright, red, curly hair. From "My Angria and the Angrians, By Lord

Charles Albert Florian Wellesley October 13th 1834." In CA EW 2, (2) 239, 245.

113 **And so on.** CA EW 2, (2) 248–49, 250.

115 **Father did not read.** In "'The Life of . . . Alexander Percy . . .' by John Bud." N WPBB II, 111–12.

116 **"Terrible" for her.** N WPBB II, 616–17.

116 **Dramatically voiced.** CB to EN, Letters I, 156.

116 **The correspondence of thinking.** JE 265, 258–59.

117 **Now we see.** JE 258.

118 **His debauched friends.** JB 323, 337.

118 **"Habitual scowl."** HG 215.

119 **Name with "infamy."** HG 219, 226, 233, 247.

120 **Unbridgeable divide.** HG 234, 242, 245, 258.

120 **On July 31, 1845.** JE 274.

121 **Life of her brother.** CB to EN, Letters I, 412.

122 **An early death.** CB to MW, Letters I, 447–48.

122 **When Charlotte imagined.** JE 121–22.

124 **Later in Mr. Rochester.** CA EW 2 (2), 92–93.

125 **Adaptations of this figure.** John Milton, *Paradise Lost*, ed. Roy Flannigan (New York: Macmillan, 1993) Book I, 54–58, 600–4.

126 **Innocent young governess.** George Gordon Lord Byron, *Lord Byron: The Major Works*, ed. Jerome J. McGann (Oxford: Oxford University Press, 2000). "The Giaour," 180, lines 180–86; 229, lines 832–35, 837–41.

127 **Anticipates Rochester's whip.** JE 419–20.

127 **"Willing to die" for him.** HG 383–84. CB to EN, Letters I, 187.

128 **Lording it over her.** HG 394.

128 **A simple "Yes."** HG 431, 432–33, 433, 434.

129 **Release and fulfillment.** HG 383–84.

CHAPTER SEVEN

131 **Ethical question in *Jane Eyre*.** WG 574.

131 **The finest motives.** EG 171.

132 **"Insular ideas about dress."** EG 174–75, 176–77.

132 **Mr. Rochester appearing.** CB to EN, Letters I, 284–85.

133 **Something she found impressive.** EG 505.

135 **Subsequent feelings for Heger.** EG 512–13.

136 **Its aching growth.** CB to EN, Letters I, 315.

136 **Village of Morton.** CB to EN, Letters I, 341.

137 **Was amply justified.** WG 264.

137 Feelings that it impels. CB to CH, Letters I, 357–58.

138 Her mode of life. JB 524.

138 In the third surviving letter. JE 149, 154.

138 Herself to hope for. CB to CH, Letters I, 379.

139 Change that reality. CB to CH, Letters I, 436.

141 More fulfilling. CB TP 102–3.

141 Years at Roe Head. CB TP 109.

141 Has never experienced. CB TP 110, 112, 114.

141 We might call this. JE 215–16.

142 Gives her a new life. CB TP 123.

142 Men they desire. CB TP 125–26.

142 "Mon maître!" CB TP 135, 141.

143 Their final reconciliation. CB TP 187–89, 210.

144 But in their first evening. JE 102, 106.

145 Pages on "The Nest." Here we will read the English translation of Charlotte's essay and Heger's comments found in Lonoff.

145 "Unity, perspective, and effect." Lonoff 40, 42.

146 As Rochester sorts. JE 106–8.

147 "Washed or torn." In *Paradise Lost* IV, 196, Satan first enters Paradise "like a Cormorant" seeking his prey, Adam and Eve. It is important to note that Charlotte had copied Bewick's illustration of this bird in January of 1829. Catalogue # 14, 160, which also discusses, page 161, the link to Jane Eyre's watercolor.

147 In the third. JE 107.

147 While Jane names. JE 108.

148 "Scarcely an interval." Kingly Crown: another allusion to *Paradise Lost* II, 673, where "the shape which shape had none" (107) is the figure of Death. Letters I, Appendix, 603.

148 Certainly Rochester. JE 108.

149 The house party scenes. JE 149.

150 Hiding in the "sanctum." JE 149.

151 Expected to fulfill. WG 147–48. Letters I, Appendix, 596. CB to EN, Letters I, 193, 191.

151 Rochester, knowing. JE 145.

151 Bases her judgments. CB *High Life* 6.

151 Jane, from the corner. JE 146, 147.

152 Brontë had been exploring. JE 153.

153 Cannot even understand. HG 239, 238–39, 242. For a more complete discussion of this character see Chapter Five. Byron, *Major Works* 247.

153 Taking Jane aside. JE 154.

154 Made of sterner stuff. CB *High Life*, 15, 17, 18.

CHAPTER EIGHT

156 **Seek revenge.** CB to HC, Letters I, 236–37. The central and indispens-
able discussion of the influence on Brontë of this extensive literature
and the pictorial illustrations that often accompanied texts is Christine
Alexander's "That Kingdom of Gloom: Charlotte Brontë, the Annuals,
and the Gothic," *Nineteenth Century Literature* 47, no. 4 (1993): 409–
36. The justly celebrated essay by Robert B. Heilman, "Charlotte
Brontë's 'New' Gothic" (in *From Jane Austen to Joseph Conrad*, ed. Robert C. Rathburn and Martin Steinmann, Jr. [Minneapolis: University
of Minneapolis Press, 1958], 118–32) is not so much about the tradition
of gothic novels but rather an argument that Brontë creates a new kind
of gothic, which he describes as dominated by "an almost violent devot-
edness that has in it at once a fire of independence, a spiritual energy, a
vivid sexual responsiveness, and, along with this, self-righteousness, a
sense of power, sometimes self-pity and envious competitiveness. To an
extent the heroines are 'unheroined,' unsweetened. Into them there has
come a new sense of the dark side of feeling and personality," 119.

156 **"Winning sweetness."** Finished December 18, 1830. CA EW I, 319, 320.

157 **Three weeks later.** CA EW I, 321.

157 **The servants insult him.** CA EW I, 321, 323.

157 **"Through the heart."** CA EW I, 322, 323.

158 **From the early tale.** JE 146–47, 187, 260, 250.

158 **Charlotte Brontë was, by dramatic contrast.** JE 251.

159 **Her tiny self with her adversaries.** EG 76. CB TP 74.

160 **In Rochester's telling.** JE 249.

161 **His "distended nostrils."** JE 400–1. Much later in the novel Rochester
remembers secretly observing Jane lapsing into "a deep reverie" where
she dreams a "day vision" that pleases her, only to be interrupted by
Mrs. Fairfax "speaking to a servant in the hall . . . " JE 267. The pattern
of this scene exactly replicates Charlotte's experience.

161 **Brontë spurns the other.** CB to BB, Letters I, 317. CB to EB, Letters
I, 329.

162 **Soon to fall in love.** CB TP 84, 85.

162 **Rochester's bitter narrative.** JE 120–21, 123, 124.

163 **Or are they?** Clare Hartwell, Nikolaus Pevsner, and Elizabeth Wil-
liamson, *The Buildings of England: Derbyshire* (New Haven, CT: Yale
University Press, 2016), 291. *Ox Comp* 347.

163 **"What a fury."** JE 9, 179, 91, 93.

165 **Locked third-floor door.** Sigmund Freud, "The Uncanny," in *On Cre-
ativity and the Unconscious*, trans. Alix Strachey, ed. Benjamin Nelson
(New York: Harper & Row, 1958) 123–24, 129, 148.

165 **Twice Jane Eyre tries.** JE 11, 242, 244, 14, 242.

165 While Jane is physically small. JE 22, 23, 30, 31, 197, 204, 250, 9.

168 Think her insane. CB to EN, Letters I, 153, 509. CB to BB, Letters I, 317.

169 Refusing to reply. HG 452. CB to EB, Letters I, 191. CB to EN, Letters I, 194, 193, 253.

170 Jane's similar outbursts. CB to EN, Letters I, 148, 399.

170 Bertha's silent intrusion. JE 245.

171 And it doesn't. JE 272.

CHAPTER NINE

172 *Jane Eyre* is a linear novel. JE 274.

173 The desperation. JE 252.

173 Brussels for good. JB 78.

174 Bleak, vacant, desolate. CB to EN, Letters I, 503.

174 Thus, Jane Eyre finds herself. JE 275, 276.

176 Society of family and friends. Letters I, Appendix, 601.

177 No need for another heaven. EG 109. Letters I, Appendix, 598. Brontë, *Wuthering Heights*, 63, 258.

177 But Jane wakes the next morning hungry. JE 277.

177 Her solitary daughter. Patrick Brontë, *Brontëana: The Rev. Patrick Brontë, His Collected Works and Life*, ed., J. Horsefall Turner (Bingley: T. Harrison & Sons, 1898), 42.

177 "Hopeless of the future." JE 277.

178 "Heart worn down by care." N PPBB 276–77.

178 There is a kind of literary model. JE 277.

178 "Requirements, and pains, and responsibilities". James Hogg, *Private Memoirs and Confessions of a Justified Sinner* (Harmondsworth: Penguin, 1983), 228.

178 Driven by hunger. JE 279, 278, 280, 285.

180 For what has happened. CB to EN, Letters I, 231.

180 There are elements. JE 280.

181 "Comfort a very desolate heart." CB to EN, Letters I, 324–25, 327, 325.

182 During this crisis. CB to EJB, Letters I, 329, 330.

182 "To an excess." CB to EN, Letters I, 334.

183 "Never more endure to see him." CB to EN, Letters I, 521.

CHAPTER TEN

185 "Our grey half-inhabited house." CB to EJB, Letters I, 331.

186 Their characters long for. "It is thought that the Diary Papers, written

by Emily and Anne, were modeled on Byron's early journal scribble in a schoolbook at Harrow and described in Moore's *Life.*" *Ox Comp* 115. Letters I, 263, note 1 quotes Shorter describing his acquisition of the Diary Papers for 1841 and 1845 and his understanding of the practice. JB 257–58.

187 Constant in her thinking. N CBP 309.

187 "Vanish into vacancy." CB to EN, Letters I, 497. N CBP 309.

188 The home Jane reaches. JE 282, 283, 285.

188 Tabby's daily chores. Letters I, Appendix, 598.

188 Patrick Brontë's chronic fear. JE 293.

189 A desk much like Charlotte's. Letters I, Appendix, 599.

189 But what most importantly strikes. JE 283.

189 Immediately Jane recognizes. JE 283, 300.

189 Brontë is clear. JE 187.

190 Jane Eyre throughout their lives. *Ox Comp* 324.

190 In the days that follow. JE 290.

191 "Fine lady anywhere else." WG 21. EG 110. CB to EN, Letters I, 206.

191 During her first glimpse. JE 283.

191 Sensed a kinship with them too. EB Diary Paper 30 July 1841, Letters I, 262–63.

192 The parsonage garden at Haworth. JE 298.

192 Seem to agree. EN in Letters I, Appendix, 601.

192 On that first night, the Rivers family. JE 287.

193 Jane, at this moment, is quite like them. CB to HC, Letters I, 241.

193 Jane Eyre soon becomes the new member. JE 298, 293, 298.

193 Jane likes to sit. JE 299.

193 The uncanny sympathies. JE 299.

194 Way for herself as well. CB to HN, Letters I, 255.

194 And then she crowns that level. JE 326, 328, 329, 330.

195 Precedence over financial matters. CB to MW, Letters I, 448.

196 "Her own way through life." CB to MW, Letters I, 448.

196 Jane's reply is the climactic conclusion. JE 333.

197 When they first meet. JE 297, 304.

198 When he sees it in Jane Eyre. CB to HN, Letters I, 185. CB to EN, Letters I, 187.

198 Charlotte's St. John Rivers. Footnote 7 in Letters I, 326. CB to EN, Letters I, 325.

199 In considering the life of Miss Wooler. CB to EN, Letters I, 187, 152.

199 That tragic year of 1842. CB to EN, Letters I, 222, 223.

200 "Specimens of the 'coarser sex.'" CB to EN, Letters I, 483.

201 "Fury cannot change my mind." N CBP 290.

201 A second poem. JE 310, 345, 299, 300.

202 Soon followed by death. N CBP 292, 294.

202 A third poem. JE 339.

202 Falls back dead. N CBP 311, 312.

202 *Jane Eyre* exactly. JE 357, 358.

CHAPTER ELEVEN

205 She had never enjoyed. CB to WSW, Letters II, 23.

205 Breaking free from St. John Rivers' demands. JE 359.

206 The deeply—and secretly. JE 360, 361.

207 At this point the close parallels. JE 361.

207 The fiery destruction. JE 365.

208 Interconnection between emotion and destruction. Letters I, Appendix, 599. JB 1007.

209 Published both at his own expense. Charlotte and her two older sisters had just been enrolled in the Cowan Bridge School a month earlier. Brontë, *Brontëana*, 212. JB 151–52.

210 "Will sink in liquid fire." Brontë, *Brontëana*, 204–8.

210 From her childhood Charlotte. JE 365.

210 Thornfield is now nothing. JE 361, 366.

212 Invalid stuck in the Haworth parsonage. JB 609. HG 233

212 Charlotte has Jane. JE 370–71.

212 While Charlotte had. JE 378.

212 As Rochester recovers partial eyesight. JE 380.

213 "Reconcilement to my Maker." Brontë, *Brontëana*, 218.

213 Thus, in a peculiarly ironic return. JE 383, 384.

EPILOGUE

216 "They appear to me in sickness and suffering." CB to WSW, Letters II, 224.

216 Secret history was thus continuing. CB to EG, Letters II, 288. CB to WSW, Letters II, 376.

217 "Name of 'Currer Bell.'" JB 743.

217 "And likely to be lonely." CB to EN, Letters III, 63.

217 "Shirley," ETC." CB to WSW, Letters III, 72. CB to GS, Letters III, 74.

218 Refused to see her. WG 571.

219 "Suddenly blood-shot." CB to EN, Letters I, 551. CB to EN, Letters III, 93.

219 They were married. CB to EN, Letters III, 95. CB to EN, Letters III, 149. CB to EN, Letters III, 168.

220 **Assiduously cared for her wellbeing.** CB to MW, Letters III, 276. CB to C. Winkworth, Letters III, 279–80. CB to EN, Letters III, 282.

220 **"My dear boy."** CBN to EN, Letters III, 283. CB to EN, Letters III, 306.

221 **"Not strong enough for marriage."** CB to EN, Letters III, 319. WG 562. A. B. Nicholls to EN, Letters III, 324. CB to Ameila Taylor, Letters III, 327. CBN to Laetitia Wheelwright, Letters III, 325. WG 564, 566.

221 **Lived to December 3, 1906.** WG 567.

222 **Violent, painful, and in itself real.** CB to GS, Letters III, 77. HG 234. HG 258.

223 **Eloquent and urgent imagination.** CB TP 3. N CBP 328.

223 **Had concealed.** Orel 84.

Index